A Church Fully Alive

A CHURCH FULLY ALIVE:

St. Irenaeus and the Praxis of Community

By Richard S. Gariepy

Original M.A. Thesis Title:
THE HERMENEUTICAL PRAXIS OF THE 'RULE OF FAITH' AS
GENERATING AN ECCLESIOLOGY OF COMMUNITY IN
IRENAEUS OF LYONS

Concordia University, Montreal, 2001 (2013)
© Richard S. Gariepy

© 2013 by the author of this book and StrongTower Community. The book author retains sole copyright to his or her contributions to this book.

ISBN: 0612640361

Cover Painting detail: *The Last Supper* by Duccio di Buoninsegna (1255-1319)
temprera on panel 1308-11 at Museo dell'Opera Metropolitana del Duomo, Siena. The work is linked to Matthew 20:26

The Blurb-provided layout designs and graphic elements are copyright Blurb Inc., 2012. This book was created using the Blurb creative publishing service. The book author retains sole copyright to his or her contributions to this book.

CONTENTS

Introduction..2

PART I: *Historical Notions of Ecclesial Community and Faith in Irenaeus Theology*

Chapter 1: **Origins of Irenaeus Theology**
Jesus—And His Disciples..12
New Testament Communities—
    In the Discipleship of Jesus..................................15
Pauline and Johannine—Influences.........................22

Chapter 2: **Notions of Community and Faith in Irenaeus**
The Life—Of Irenaeus...42
The Works—Of Irenaeus...45
The Role—Of 'The Rule of Faith'...............................47
The Role—Of 'Ecclesial Community'........................51

PART II: *Contemporary Perspectives on Irenaeus Incarnational Paradigm
for Church as Community of Faith*

Chapter 3: **Frameworks in which to Interpret Irenaeus Ideas of How to Build up the Ecclesial Community**
The Hermenutical Praxis—
    As the 'Rule of Faith/Truth'..................................66
The Praxis of Eastern Orthodoxy—
    Living the Faith...72
Sociological-Historical Praxis Notions—
    Of Christian Morality and Community...............79
'Koinonia' Praxis—
    The 'Communal Ethic' as Biblical Norm..............86

Chapter 4: Four Contemporary Paradigms Based on Irenaeus Theology as Central to his notions of Church as 'Community and Faith'

The Self in the Body—
    Selfhood and Community...96
Creation and Cosmos—
    The 'Cosmic Christ' and Creation Mystics...................100
Growth Education in Divinity—
    And the Future of Humankind.....................................105
The Ecumenical Unity of the Church—
    Ecclesial Orthopraxis...110

Conclusion---
    Eucharist as the Ultimate 'Hermeneutic of Praxis'
   124

Bibliography..132

CONCORDIA UNIVERSITY

Abstract:
THE HERMENEUTICAL PRAXIS OF THE 'RULE OF FAITH' AS GENERATING AN ECCLESIOLOGY OF COMMUNITY IN IRENAEUS OF LYONS
by Richard S. Gariepy
Thesis Advisor: Professor Dr. Charles Kannengiesser
Department of Theology

Introduction: 'The Glory of God is a living person...a church community fully alive.' A modern paraphrase of Irenaeus famous dictum or a rediscovery of a profound insight? Can we build a continuity with the relevance of modern day paradigms from how Irenaeus saw his world and how we see our world, especially as it relates to being human and experiencing church?

Specifically, in *Part I,* we will focus on aspects of the historical, dialectical and, doctrinal ways of communicating how Irenaeus viewed personal salvation and the church as related to community and faith-lifestyle notions (what has been called the 'tradition' of the church and the 'rule of faith'). We will seek to incorporate recent insights in the sociology of knowledge that have helped reorientate our perspective on a communal ethic in the early period of Christian ecclesiology.

In rediscovering his major theological paradigms of Life, Incarnation, and Deification through a 'church faith and community' prism, *Part II* will seek to draw out four modern aspects of this historical dialectic of Irenaeus' theology that are central to church as 'community' and integrally related to 'faith as lifestyle.' Namely, what could be called his sub-paradigmal themes of: 'Creation and cosmos', 'growth education in divinity', the 'Body of Christ and the flesh of selfhood', and finally, the 'ecumenical freedom of unity as church ecclesia'. We will see how all of this is incorporated in a definition of what I call, the hermeneutical praxis, or orthopraxis theology of Irenaeus and his use of the 'rule of faith (truth)' as generating a communal ecclesiology.

Acknowledgments

The author wishes to thank the Faculty of Theology when it was at the Loyola Campus of Concordia University for its tenacious persistence over the years which has allowed me to begin studies in 1976 and finish them in 2001 (there was a break in the middle!). A special mention of appreciation goes to a very dear 'couple' of International repute, and the first Patristic Scholars I have ever had the pleasure to be aquatinted with in Dr. Pamela Bright and Dr. Charles Kannengiesser—whose encouragement, inspiration, and patience, allowed me to complete this thesis and to whom I have dedicated it.

As well, special mention must go to my good friend Professor Russell Moroziuk, now retired from our faculty, whose influence made me realize the enjoyment of the art of theological dialogue and who made me sensitive to the Eastern Orthodox way and insight into the Irenaeus perspective.

And finally, a note of gratitude to the late Canon Dr. Jan H. L. Dijkman, former Rector, of the Church of St. James the Apostle, who provided me with the crucial time and support for the final completion of this thesis.

INTRODUCTION

God gave breath to the first human being to bring the whole body to life, and He has given His new "breath," the Holy Spirit, to the Church, for the same purpose—that every member of the body should come alive. The Spirit is our link with Christ...All the means through which the Holy Spirit works are within the Church—that is why the Church is a living body.

—Irenaeus of Lyon1

    It has always been an interest of mine to examine the explicit role of 'faith and community' on institutional and ecclesiastical structures as part of the renewal process and origins or vitality of the Christian tradition today and in history. In reflecting on the thesis proposal for an FCAR research scholarship, I stated it as a need to examine a predominant sociological and ecclesiological norm present in our society—as the rediscovery of the role and relevance of 'basic communities'. What is also interesting, are the many factors facilitating this process, whether philosophical/technological (it didn't seem that long ago that a 1996 Christmas issue of Time magazine's cover theme was on 'Jesus and the Internet'!), political, economic or cultural, and as was evidenced in recent history around the world with the budding 1960's communitarian movement in North America, the Latin America 'communidades Eclesiasis de Base', or European Socialist experiments, for example. As I have observed, all these developments have two factors in common, namely, their struggle for the marginalized and oppressed, and their need for community structures either in societal transition or towards societal transformation.

    In examining the formative period of the New Testament Church, especially in the Pauline Epistles, the Acts of the Apostles, and the Johannine communities which were coming to be called 'church' (regardless of the language or imagery used), one notes that ecclesiological structures and communitarian notions mutually affected one another. The question becomes particularly important in regards to the post-canonical writings and early Patristic documents related to the early Christian Church, a time when Christianity struggled to survive and grow in late Greco-Roman society (in some ways, a time not unlike our own).

It is my concern to focus on this period of the 'undivided church' and in particular the writings of Irenaeus of Lyons, not only because of this crucial time period for ecclesial Christianity but also to explore, what I call the 'Irenaen Life paradigm' ('The Glory of God is a living man [sic]; and the life of man in beholding God' *A.H.* 4.7) for today. Whereas Irenaeus has been portrayed as staunch defender of 'The Faith' and upholder of a rigid 'Apostolic Succession', there is today a reappraisal and new appreciation for the notions of a *Patristic praxis or orthopraxis*, in relation to doctrine *and lifestyle* as a more organic inter-related *communal ethic*. A crucial question then becomes: How did Irenaeus see his context (or religious cultural matrix) in relation to 'faith and community' as church in his day? And its continuity: How do we make the transition and insight to today? Another way I put the question is, 'How did the historical/theological notion of dialectic affect in Irenaeus, his understanding of ecclesiological structure as manifested in local church communities *resulting from their faith-lifestyles or rule of faith*?'

Associated with this research topic are the manifest themes of second century Christianity, of what it means to be human and divine, the beginning of specific views of authority and Apostolic tradition, of controversies and persecutions as defining faith expression and Church community. It is to attempt to first, look historically and then ultimately, sociologically, at the theological definition and role of 'grass roots' base communities in ecclesiological development *and* the renewal of society.

The theology of Irenaeus' which insists that the life of being human is the Glory of God is integrally connected in a two clause statement with the aim and goal of the Christian life and prayer as seeing or visioning God. This has profound implications. It becomes evident that if the goal towards which human life needs to move is the realization of our Godlikeness in a living relationship with God which is finally vision—the union of the human and the divine which is a fact in the person of Christ—then it becomes a task to be achieved for human beings at large. And it is God's gesture of love in becoming human as both the *sign* of our destiny and the *source* of the only means of its fulfillment.

This conviction is expressed in Irenaeus simple and bold formula that Jesus Christ our Lord, God's Word, 'on account of his measureless love became what we are that he might make us in the end what he is' (5, pref.). It is the insistence upon a deification process of transformation as a process of growth and maturation. Like all his language it is in biblical imagery, and the precondition is that it should occur with the right use of a person's freedom. Irenaeus, in common with many later Fathers and Mothers, is explicit in seeing the human capacity for free choice as a primary mark of our godliness and its connection with the true nature of love (*A.H.*4.37.1). Thus Irenaeus sees God as still at work on the making of human beings.

There must therefore, have been an influence on how Irenaeus viewed the primacy of a faith lifestyle or rule, *and* church community, explicitly or implicitly through his theology, his pastoral praxis, and approach to ministry.

Irenaeus' 'Against Heresies' is fundamentally an 'exposition of the faith' as it exists in inter-relationship to Scripture, tradition and the Church. It is my conviction as stated similarly in Barbara Ellen Bowe's study of 1Clement,[2] "that an exaggerated emphasis on the question of ecclesiological office has prevented a satisfactory appraisal of its whole ecclesiological perspective (i.e. a strong and urgent appeal for unity and solidarity based not on hierarchical agendas but on the conviction that Christians form a common brotherhood *adelphotes* ...[as] the core of its ecclesiology)." We will as well, examine the argument for Christian praxis (which permeates all the writings of all the Apologists) which in the ancient church was reiterated again and again as—true praxis is

Introduction

bound together profoundly with true teaching.3

The challenge is to summarize this theological rallying cry of someone who lived over 1800 years ago to today's world. So if we were to begin with our 'common experience' or more formally stated—a theological contemporary approach, we would tend to begin with an anthropological perspective and then move unto the theological soteriology. But if we are to understand how the thought of Irenaeus moves historically, we must work with his starting point which is not anthropological but Christological. It is an approach which faithfully reflects the ancient church (or actually the still then rather primitive praxis church perception) which says in effect, 'This is who Jesus is, and what he did for us; see what that must mean for who we are and how we live' (issuing in a personal faith and communitarian response). For central to early Christian thought is the conviction that Jesus Christ is the principle of interpretation of human experience. We are thus speaking first historically, at how Irenaeus theologically looked at ecclesiology, and secondly, to situate it within a study of the correlatives of soteriology and then anthropology.

We will thus touch on the dialectic of the historical theological praxis issues which confronted Irenaeus and helped define his 'foundational faith stance' in his controversy primarily with the Gnostic heresies.

We are then in a better position to appreciate the context to our own times. Raymond Brown, in a concluding reflection of his book *The Community of the Beloved Disciple*, saw parallels with certain perennial church problems in the Johannine Gospel and Epistles (a heritage Irenaeus considered himself to be a part of) and our own times. Namely, that struggle between Churches over a diversity of traditions within an individual church, tend to follow the same lines over the centuries. And part of this familiar pattern, is the anguish over authoritarian church offices and the reluctant recognition, especially with groups committed to the freedom under the Spirit, like the Johannine community (and the Irenaen also?), that some form of authority is the only way to protect church communities from unbalanced and extravagant claims in the name of the Spirit. But where does the creative tension lay?

As Sir Edwyn Hoskyns states in a similar vein: "The modern reader will therefore not apprehend the Fourth Gospel as its author meant it to be apprehended if he concludes that it was against, say Gnosticism, or Docetism, or Ebiontism, or even against the Jews, and rests satisfied with the explanation, without at the same time recognizing that those ancient movements of religion are still deep-seated and destructive factors in *our common life.*" [emphasis mine]4

Thus, I will also seek to explore several insights rooted in Irenaeus, which after having entered into how the man himself viewed the situation, we will attempt to develop possible connections to relevant contemporary faith-lifestyle and communitarian Church experiences.5

Part of the definition of my thesis question in consultation with my thesis advisor Dr. Charles Kannengiesser, has focused on three questions asked in the light of my focus: 1) What was Irenaeus attitude toward bodily existence of human beings? (as shown for example through his texts, phrases, and places alluding to his optimistic answers); how did he present or see Gnostics; and refuse to see a dualistic understanding of body/flesh? And 2) How and why does Irenaeus emphasize human freedom? This is to be linked with the first question and opens all sorts of ethical issues, and community life virtues. Irenaeus insisted strongly on freedom because of his notion of universal creation, i.e., what is proper to human beings in the whole cosmos is to be free, unique beings created free. What is peculiar to Irenaeus was his conceiving the creation of the human species—as a state of infancy, so that the view of the relationship of human beings and the creator implies a divine education, and a response of human beings to this divine education. Thus the cosmos can be viewed as good.

Most importantly, the above two questions feed into 3) How did 'The Rule of Faith' generate ecclesial community? Developing a fruitful and consistent view along with the prior two questions, in

Introduction

turn focuses our attention on certain types of community, not as moralistic but as a Christian past tied to the original foundations of a Christian faith heading toward a dynamic fulfillment. Thus, it is a Church open geographically, not closed up or sectarian, (in this sense what is catholic of Irenaeus is truly small 'c'), but ready to communicate with communities of different types.

I will seek, finally to draw out from our three questions, four contemporary paradigm aspects of Irenaeus' theology that are central to our main theme of church community ushering out of a faith lifestyle (which will be seen to be integrally related to Irenaeus' Rule of Faith and his ecclesiology). Namely, 'Creation and the cosmos', 'growth education in divinity', the 'Body of Christ and the flesh of selfhood', and lastly, the ecumenical 'unity of church ecclesia' as all related to an orthopraxis theology of Irenaeus. These I believe are fundamental dialectical-dialogical contexts for exploring as modern paradigms, the tradition of the ecclesiological dimension of faith community in our time, and Irenaeus.

NOTES

1. Translation by David Winter in *After the Gospels* (Mowbrays: London, 1977) p.76
2. Barbara Ellen Bowe, *A Church in Crisis: Ecclesiology and Paraenesis in Clement of Rome* (Fortress Press: Mineapolis, 1988) p. 4
3. Gerhard Lohfink, *Jesus and Community: The Social Dimension of Christian Faith* (Fortress Press: Philadelphia, 1984) p.175
4. E.C. Hoskyns, *The Fourth Gospel* (Faber and Faber: London, 1947) p. 49
5. Gregory Baum in an article on "The Church" (Grail Vol. Issue I) talks about a new way of seeing Church Ecclesiology promoted at Vatican Council II by the Belgian Bishop Emile Joseph De Smedt in a popular book that was called The Priesthood of the Faithful. It countered the old hierarchical top-down notion of Church as institution. It speaks for a rediscovery of a notion of a more democratized leadership as exemplified in a renewal of scholarly thinking regarding the Early Church Fathers, and as I will try to show in Irenaeus in particular. See for example J.H. McDonald's *The Crucible of Christian Morality: Religion in the First Christian Centuries*(1998), John Breck's *The Power of the Word* (1986), Howard Kee's *Who Are the People of God: Early Christian Models of Community* (1995), and Barbara Bowe's *A Church in Crisis: Ecclesiology and Paraenesis in Clement of Rome* (1998).

To show how we have come full circle, De Smedt argued that the movement of contemporary ecclesiology speaks a need for a more popular, communitarian imagination which reflects a closer self-understanding of the early Church (recorded in many passages of the New Testament). Here is the testimony of the apostles, inspired by the Spirit, that brought together those who believed in the Christ reality. In receiving the Spirit of God they were adapted as the People of God which together constituted the Church. God's self-communication took place in the hearts of the faithful and in the communities constituted by them. It was to protect and intensify the divine presence of Jesus Christ in their midst, that the Church was graced with the sacred ministry of apostolic origin. That is, through the service of bishops and priests, the fraternal community entered more deeply into communion with the Spirit. God's self-disclosure takes place among the base of the people as Church, and the task of ministry is to help people share more deeply in the divine gifts.

The bishop's bold proposals, which where eventually integrated into the ecclesiological texts of Vatican II, stated that all Christians participate in the three-fold ministry of Jesus Christ: as prophet uttering divine truth; as priest offering acceptable worship in his own self-surrender; and as king when Jesus served, mediated and anticipated God's approaching reign. Christians participate in this three-fold ministry because they too have a prophetic task in uttering the truth and handing on the revealed message;

they have a priestly task when they offer Eucharistic worship and surrender themselves to God; and Christians have a share in Christ's kingship as they serve God's coming reign by mediating God's power in overcoming of the world's sin. What is the task of the ordained ministry n the Church? If all are priests, what is the role of the ordained? As we have intimated already, De Smedt says, it is not to replace the threefold ministry of the faithful, but in a special way to promote and protect this ministry. The power of the hierarchy is a service, an enabling ministry; it is to testify to the truth and hand on the Christian message. The ordained hierarchy (or leadership structures) does not replace but seeks to enhance the teaching function of the Christian people. The ordained hierarchy celebrates the sacramental liturgy, it does not replace but enhance the priesthood of the baptized. The ordained hierarchy participates in Christ's kingship, serves God's coming reign, and wrestles against the obstacles of sin and evil. Yet these activities do not replace but enhance the share in Christ's kingship given to all believers.

PART I:

HISTORICAL NOTIONS OF ECCLESIAL FAITH AND COMMUNITY IN IRENAEUS THEOLOGY

Chapter 1

ORIGINS OF IRENAEUS THEOLOGY

We will look at the possible Pauline and Johannine ecclesiological influences (and the primary influence in turn, of Jesus understanding of the social dimension of His calling) on Irenaeus' theology and examine the perennial struggle against counter-community pressures, such as Gnosticism, on the Church throughout history. This is already seen in St. Paul and St. John's Epistles in its early stages and the misunderstood and pernicious tendencies felt on Christian communities, seen as seductive knowledge, the confusion of believers, and the spreading of dangerous forms of pluralism within the 'unity of the faith'. These foundations will help answer the question in the next chapter, 'How did Irenaeus combat these inauthentic theologies in his faith communities?'

Our search with Irenaeus is for a sense of his notion of ecclesia as seen through the prism of faith and community, i.e., faith community. It is a seeking for what I call his 'hermenutical praxis' and a key to ascertaining the emphasis on his orthopraxis theology and understanding of Church.1 It is the importance of discerning, I believe, an implied communal ethic, that is generated by his ecclesiology. I will in turn try to show that it was fostered by certain major biblical influences, not the least of which was the originator of our faith, Jesus, and *his* notion of discipleship community that accompanied it. We will do the same by way of the Pauline and Johannine traditions and view a symbiosis process of influence at work on Irenaeus.

Jesus—And His Disciples

According to William P. Lowe, Irenaeus' text "points to the praxis of Christian discipleship as the foundational hermenutical base from which he operates." If he is correct, we can proceed to inquire into how Irenaeus' text thematizes the commitments which govern that praxis and which shape as well, the intentional faith community in which his truth story invites his readers to inhabit.2 We can then ask of what values Irenaeus' work seeks to mediate. Can we say the same about Jesus? Can we even see a similar theme in the Johannine tradition (as we shall see shortly), which would go back to Jesus through this same discipleship theme and the resultant emphasis on Christian faith ecclesial community that ultimately influenced Irenaeus?

Theologian Gerhard Lohfink too sees one of the main characteristics of Jesus mission as forming a circle of disciples.3 There were basically two groups in Israel which heard Jesus and believed in Him. There were those who accepted Jesus message, but remained where they were in whatever town or village awaiting the reign of God (Mark 5:19-20) throughout the country. On the other hand, there were disciples (Greek *mathetes*) in the stricter sense who were distinguished from the followers, who were more like the rabbinic teacher-student relationship. To follow Jesus was to mean to do so quite literally.

So we cannot escape the fact that Jesus was the center of the life of a small community with a band of various followers. John's Gospel (1:35-51) narrates for us Jesus' first contact with the Apostles: "come and see." This circle of disciples who followed Jesus was a firmly fixed group. We see the evident attractiveness of Jesus' human warmth for them. Throughout the Gospel we see a series of interpersonal relationships which He had with a small group of "disciples." Life was learned by living with Jesus, not by theoretical study (although there are many instances of teaching and applied learning). Jesus began His work by forming a community and later gradually giving them the message and inviting their response and commitment. He called them to a discipleship which required that they give up their prior occupations and leave their families (cf. Mk. 1:16-20). This common life meant more than merely being with a teacher, listening and observing Him, or to learn the Torah from Jesus statements and manner of life. There is a sense in which this discipleship community life was a "community of destiny," says

Lohfink. They had to be prepared to suffer what Jesus suffered, even if it meant persecution or execution.

These were radical demands. They were to represent Israel "symbolically" as a whole (not individualistically) accepting Jesus message: of complete dedication to the Gospel of the reign of God, radical conversion to a new way of life, and a gathering unto a community of brothers and sisters. They were to prefigure the eschatological people of God with whom Jesus was concerned and what Israel was meant to become.

There are those who see close parallels with today's base communities, which entails giving responsibility to other members of the group to share the work of the leaders' vision.[4] Jesus respected and made use of their previous friendships and blood relationships. As leader He also shared the life and work experiences of the group. The disciples followed a person, not a doctrine. He developed quality time with a select few members of the community, yet it was not limited to the Twelve (and perhaps their wives), but was open to many others and the multitudes, whose numbers the Gospels do not give us.

The character of Jesus' community is marked for instance, by baptismal beginnings (a sense of mission), preaching, combat with the demonic and sickness, the priority of the " lost sheep of Israel," a confronting of persecution, coming together for common prayer, mutual forgiveness, and rejecting excommunication of public sinners without having tried to call them to repentance. Certain other aspects of Jesus life with His group also seem to be significant, such as simplicity of life and lack of bureaucratic structures, which He would critique if they were not faithful to the heart of the issue, in matters human and spiritual. Jesus group of disciples can be seen to be dynamically creative in terms of the renewal of human interrelations.

Lohfink states a survey of the synoptic tradition that shows how strongly Jesus was concerned with community.[5] Jesus was especially concerned with the "people of Israel," the "gathered" and "restored." It was an eschatological thrust of the concept of "gathering the people of God." The reign of God in its final form can be seen in Jesus as a universal reality which transcended theIsrael of the day. But it was precisely to the degree that the people of God let itself be grasped by God's rule, that it would be transformed. That is, it would become a "contrast-society," it would become a family of brothers and sisters, like the family Jesus had gathered in His circle of disciples. The will of Jesus was for community, of different social relations obtained within it (as an actual circle of disciples) than the rest of society. There would be no retribution; no structures of domination or violence. We are dealing here with a concrete social reality, not some "ideal community" or "hidden society."

New Testament Communities — In the Discipleship of Jesus

We can see some of the above qualities manifesting in the early Church. Most of the early Churches were domestic Churches meeting in the homes of the members. It was true because of their limited size and the persecution they experienced. It was also the influence of the dominant cultural mode of the Greco-Roman society adapted by the early Church.6 But the experience of meeting in homes continued even when the persecution ended. Prayer and worship was central to all their experiences. States Russell:

> The households organized in response to the reality of Jesus Christ were often multilingual, multicultural, and from the very beginning they included the rich and poor. We also know that women exercised significant leadership in many of the new communities. The households provided a foundation for communal growth, were the locus of cultic activities such as the Eucharist, and undergirded economic sharing. Households met at sites accommodating ten to twenty people to larger sites that could hold thirty, fifty, and even a hundred. In adopting the household as its form, the early Church provided a convert with a new and primary community to which to belong, a community clearly intended to replace the primary community [family] from which the

convert came. 7

The ideal was to have Jesus as the center of their community, and he played a much larger role than any Church authority (cf. 1 Cor. 3:1-17). The very first communities shared their goods in common for a time, after which it seemed, only exceptional groups attempted to live such an ideal. The Apostles called them to a sense of community with other Churches. Each individual church community quickly developed a number of different ministries and charisms which were for the service of the group and the larger society. Ministers (most of who were lay, but new Churches had to be confirmed by the Apostles or those delegated by them) often shared the lifestyle of the people since they were generally chosen from among them. Each Church had to struggle to use the language of the people and to adapt itself to their culture and be open to all with sharing the message lived out in these communities. It was not that there weren't disputes or differences but that a personal response was demanded of members.8

Lohfink poses the question directly in terms of how the beginning eyewitnesses and immediate followers of Jesus, acted with regard to community. He lists eight primary characteristics: the Church as the People of God; the Presence of the Spirit; the elimination of social barriers; the praxis of 'togetherness'; brotherly love; the renunciation of domination; the church as contrast-society; and the sign for the nations.9 I would like to briefly comment on four as pertaining to our theme of Irenaeus on faith community.

i. *The Presence of the Spirit*

Jesus' own movement of gathering was associated with overpowering manifestations of the Spirit which occurred as well suddenly in the post-Easter community. According to the Scriptures the coming of God's Spirit is an eschatological phenomenon, described as God's gift to the eschatological community (cf. Isa. 32:15; Ezek. 11:19; 36:26-27; Joel 3:1-2; Acts 2:17-19 in terms of prophecy, visions, healings). When the reign of God becomes present, its healing power extends not only reaching deeply into human corporeality, but also extends deeply into the social dimensions existence. It must free people for new community. This is the linking of preaching and healing that was preserved in the early Church (Acts 2:43). It is impossible, says Lohfink, to discuss the self-understanding of the early Church without considering its consciousness of the living presence of the Spirit in its midst.[10] The rule of God comes not only in word but in deed. It grasps the whole of our existence and it never exists on isolated individuals. It exists for others as Jesus is always concerned with the people of God. When a Christian community accepts the Gospel, lives on the basis of the Gospel, a new reality, reaching deeply into the corporal dimension, is set free (1 Cor. 12:8; Gal. 3:1-5). The reign of God is already breaking in (Lk. 12:20), is a key eschatological event in Jesus preaching. The N.T. communities preserved this tension as the decisive experience—as a presence of the gift of salvation experienced as the eschatological Spirit poured out and active in the communities in a multitude of charisms *in the power of the Spirit* (cf. Acts 2; 13:9; 1 Cor. 12:9-10).

ii. The Praxis of "Togetherness"

We will explore this "decisive experience" of transformation in the early Christian Church from another aspect of the concept of community (or *koinonia*---which was highly significant for them in itself,[11] and which we will examine in chapter 4 on frameworks in which to interpret Irenaeus), and a closely related linguistic clue in the term "togetherness" (*allelon*).[12] This word perhaps more acurately and forcefully grasps the communal sense of ecclesial communion, states Lohfink.

Interestingly, he mentions that even though it was an important part of early Christian ecclesiology, it does not warrant an entry in Kittel and Friedrich's ten volume *Theological Dictionary of the New*

Testament. It is instructive to see the list made by Lohfink, which is far from exhaustive:

outdo one another in showing honor (Rom. 12:10)
live in harmony with one another (Rom. 12:16)
welcome one another (Rom. 5:17)
admonish one another (Rom. 15:14)
greet one another with a holy kiss (Rom. 16:16)
wait for one another (1 Cor. 11:33)
have the same care for one another (1Cor. 12:25)
be servants of one another (Gal. 5:13)
bear one another's burdens (Gal. 6:2)
comfort one another (1Thess. 5:11)
build one another up (1Thess.1:11)
be at peace with one another (1Thess. 5:13)
do good to one another (1Thess. 5:15)
bear with one another lovingly (Eph. 4:2)
be kind and compassionate to one another (Eph. 4:32)
be subject to one another (Eph. 5:21)
forgive one another (Col. 3:13)
confess your sins to one another (Jam. 5:16)
pray for one another (Jam. 5.16)
meet one another with humility (1Pet. 5:5)
have fellowship with one another (1Jn. 1:7)

We see a list here, like Jesus, Paul was concerned with the gathering or building up of the one people of God, which is in accordance with God's will. These admonitions are in the context of edifying communities of mutual accountability. Closer examination shows that what seems apparently insignificant can provide a strict criterion of the reality of community which implies a fundamental ecclesiological decision. Behind it lies ultimately Jesus' intention of leading the people of God to the true community once again.13

iii. Brotherly Love

In Mark 3:35 (cf. Matt. 23:9; Mk. 10:29-30) we see how Jesus' followers would receive a *new family*, which had an aspect of dissension on the old notion of blood family or cultural ties (Lk. 12:53). The early Church tried to remain true to Jesus on this point as well. An important role in this process was played by the early Christian Apostles and itinerant missionaries, who handed on most intensively Jesus' radical ethic of discipleship and sought to embody it in their own lives (the program of the 'new family' has been kept alive in the Church in large part by monasticism).

The early "house Churches" was where Christian brotherhood could be realized concretely. In each city where Christians lived one or more families made their homes available for the assembly, as both the center of the community life and a place of support for Christians traveling (cf. Acts 12:12; Rom. 16:5, 23; 1 Cor. 16:15,19; Col. 4:15; Phil. 2). Christians were committed to fraternal love as a concrete tangible pious moral practice based on the eschatological outpouring of the Spirit. Something of the sense of the new reality of sisterly and brotherly community which was spreading is captured in the new term coined by the early Church as *agape* (love).

An important aspect to this term is that it was not used in a universalistic sense as we do today. But most contexts of its use in the N.T. clearly refer to the believing community itself or "mutual love"[14] or togetherness (different words are used for strangers or enemy) contrary to much contemporary thought.[15] As Lohfink comments, when the N.T. speaks of interpersonal love it means almost exclusively fraternal love within the communities. The Johannine literature, in which this phenomena has always been recognized, does not stand alone. John's Gospel and Letters simply reflect with particular clarity what is true for the entire N.T. Granted Jesus expanded the boundaries of our neighbor, but what of loving one's neighbor? Did the early Church compromise here? Lohfink states that in this instance, the reality which Jesus intended with love of enemy is clearly present here in the N.T. letters, and is a challenge to society at large to emulate the example. And secondly, it is easy to misunderstand Jesus position from our undifferentiated manner of universal philanthropy. For Jesus stood within the O.T. foundation, where one's neighbor is first of all one who lives nearby and who shares the same faith.

Jesus did relativize the concept by making it clear that anyone in need becomes one's brother. But says Lohfink, this meant precisely that fraternal love which had its basic and permanent location in the people of God must extend to anyone who is in need. It is precisely in preserving this basis that makes it possible to go beyond the boundaries of the community. In this fashion an ever increasing number of people were drawn into the fraternity of the Church, and new neighborly relationships became possible.

iv. The Church as Contrast-Society

This notion of a contrast-society or counter-society is not a biblical concept, but Lohfink felt since we no longer see this reality or recognize it, he had to point it out. For it fills the Bible from beginning to end, since the people of God are always understood as contrast-society, i.e., that they are different from the national structure, of the Israel that knows they are chosen and called by God in its entire existence (including its social dimension). As Deut. 7 makes clear, the people of God is the Israel which, according to God's will, is to distinguish itself from all other peoples of the earth. This was the self-evident background to all Jesus actions. The only difference between the O.T. prophets message and Jesus, is that His message stood within an eschatological perspective, when God would restore and even reestablish His people to carry out His plan of having a holy people in the midst of the nations.

It is true that Jesus never called for a political or revolutionary transformation of Jewish society. Yet the repentance he demanded as a consequence of His preaching of the reign of God sought to ignite within the people of God a movement in comparison to which the normal type of revolution is insignificant. Jesus' call for the renunciation of violence and domination presupposed a group coming together who would take these issues seriously, and it is precisely the complex of social reality they sought to transform. Jesus also spoke bluntly in the "prayer for gathering" of 'Our Father'—as a prayer which incorporates the entire O.T. theme of holiness. And the N.T. communities also understood themselves as a fundamental contrast to paganism, as a holy people.

This question has special importance since for centuries now the Christian Churches have scarcely had the feeling of being in contrast or an alternative type of society. Yet as Eph. 5:8 says: "For once you were darkness, but now you are light in the Lord; walk as children of light." This construction is so common in the epistles that it is possible to speak of a fixed pattern which has been called the "Once and now pattern" (cf. Titus 3:3-6) of contrast. The new person in Christ is contrasted with the old person (cf. also Eph. 2:15; 4:24).

It is a renewal of mind that brings about a new creation wherever the Church has come into being as the realm of Christ's rule. This fundamental biblical principle, which we might term the "sanctity of the community", is not only being sanctified through Christ's redemptive deed, it also has to practice this sanctity through a corresponding life. This shows the sharp contrast of church and world. We sense this profound opposition only in Johannine writings (see Jn.17:14-19), but a closer inspection of Paul draws the boundary just as sharply, whether for instance in admonishing Christians to not use secular courts but settle within the community (1Cor. 6:5-7); between "believers" and "unbelievers" (1 Cor. 14:22; cf. 1 Cor. 6:1-2,6); of those "inside" (1Cor.5:12) and those "outside" (1Cor. 5:12-13; 1 Thess.4:12). So we can see this concept of the sanctification of the community has basic lines in the O.T. that continue into the New. For the Church is a holy nation (1 Pet. 2:9); it is a holy temple of God (1 Cor. 3:17); it is sanctified and purified through the baptismal bath of water

(Eph. 5:26); the faithful are sacred branches on the noble olive tree of Israel (Rom. 11:16-17); and they are called by God to holiness (1 Thess.4:3).

Pauline and Johannine Influences

Many authors speak of the major influence Paul and John had on the theological thought of Irenaeus and his biblical and Christological emphasis.16 Irenaeus was brought up in Asia Minor, where he had known Ignatius' colleague Polycarp of Smyrna. The later provided Irenaeus not only with evidence of a champion of orthodoxy and martyrdom, and who had ostensibly consorted with John and Philip and other Apostles of Jesus, but someone Irenaeus could say he had seen and heard himself as a youth. This was an important link with Irenaeus' own Gospel and idea and validation of episcopal tradition and from whom he learned of the Johannine tradition, and that living in the truth meant participation in the divine life and light—"seeing God and enjoying his generosity" (*A.H.* 4.34).17

The Pauline echoes in Irenaeus are entirely characteristic of the language of Galatians, II Corinthians and Ephesians (and especially Romans and I Corinthian's) and in large part comes naturally.18 Irenaeus who interprets the Pauline texts with the help of others, takes practically from the whole Pauline corpus. As a result we can see how Irenaeus vision of the unity of salvation history involves both restoration and continuous growth based on Pauline texts and theology.19

But I would like to focus here on Paul's notion of ecclesiology. The Christian writings of the first century reflect a variety of attitudes towards the meaning and practice of community. But it is the earliest amongst them in Paul's letters, that contain the most detailed information. According to Robert Banks, Paul was not the first to formulate the Christian idea of community, yet there can be no doubt that he gave more attention to this than anyone else during that period.20 Within the Pauline correspondence we find a rich selection of images of the Church. In everyone of his writings aspects of community life come into discussion, and in a few, it emerges as the main issue for consideration. Not that he provides any systematic treatment of the idea, for mostly he worked out his views in response to the problems of particular communities. Yet, for Banks the distinctiveness of Paul's contribution, nevertheless, is no more so than in his idea of community.[21]

Yet it was not easy for Paul in trying to build his ministry of Church community. There were those who questioned the Apostolic authority which he claimed. Paul seems to have had a running battle with them just as he had, from time to time, to make real efforts to come to terms with Jewish Christianity (the Judaizers) in general and Apostolic authorities in particular. And there were the threats coming from Gentile paganism (idolatry and immorality were key issues) and from early expressions of 'gnosis' with their extremes of asceticism and antinomianism.

Faced with such challenges, Paul had to emphasize the immediacy of his vocation—it came from Christ, without Apostolic mediation, and he appealed to the evidences of grace and of the Spirit at work in his Churches as validation of his Apostolic work. It was of prime importance that the ethos of the Churches reflected the Spirit of Christ.[22] Paul also emphasized the role of edification in his Churches defined in terms of balance, discernment, responsibility and participation, self-control, and unity in diversity among the members.[23]

i. *The Freedom of Christ: the role of the Spirit in Paul*

A proper introduction to Paul's idea of ecclesial community must include a consideration of the theological basis that supports it. Most of the different aspects of Paul's idea of community are related, for Banks, in some way or other to his understanding of freedom. Paul asserts that people are so "enslaved" by their baser inclinations that they are no longer "free" to properly pursue their real potential and destiny. This was the sin of "the first Adam" and along with it came the necessity of the law along with the power of death as part of the solidarity of the human race and the world. However a second community has now come into existence, through the achievement of that other person Paul terms "the second Adam." Through His obedience the trend initiated by the first Adam has been reversed (Rom. 5:12ff). And since He did this not for His own sake but for all as our representative, He is the foundation of a new community, humanity or creation.24

We can begin to see how closely Paul's understanding of freedom, or salvation is bound up with his idea of community. It is into a new community that Christ's reconciliation with God has brought us, however much we may experience this event as an individual affair. Those who acknowledge Jesus as having gained this victory on their behalf, and who have received His Spirit into their lives, are liberated from the things by which they were inexorably gripped beforehand. They are free from the compulsion to sin and from the tendency to rely on their own moral and religious achievements.25 And they are free from the bonds which death irrevocably puts around them (Rom. 6:23; 8:21), and from the supernatural agencies which blinded their former judgment and influenced their former choices (Rom. 8:38-39; Gal. 4:8-11).

The experience of the Spirit has reversed the effect, so that instead of being blinded and tyrannized, its 'gift of truth' and 'power of love' has released them, and for the first time granted them freedom to choose a way of life for themselves (Rom. 5:5; 1 Cor. 2:10-11). There is still a tension to live with between the mind and conscience (Rom. 7:24-25a; 1Cor. 15:53-57). But it is a freedom to grow into maturity, into "the full stature of Christ" (Eph. 4:13).

This fundamental freedom is not merely an independence *from* certain things, but also an independence *for* others. And there is a new liberty towards *God*, which dispels fear and leads to freedom in His presence of a most intimate kind (Rom. 8:15-18; Gal. 4:1-7). At a certain point Paul shows that we must drop the language of service and slavery for we are now in relationship as descriptive of a new family. It is a service to God which is quite free in character (Rom. 1:19).

This also leads to a new freedom towards *others*. This includes freedom from the fear of others' judgments as well as from one's own attempts to manipulate them (1Cor. 4:3; 9:19; 2 Cor. 11:20-21). It is also includes freedom in communicating one's thoughts, expressing one's emotions, and the opening up of one's life and the sharing of one's possessions (2 Cor. 3:12; 6:11; 7:4; 8:2; 9:13). So this freedom granted by God not only transfers men and women out of broken relations with God, and defective solidarity with society, but into a new community with both, inclining them to live the kind of life that will deepen and extend that new ecclesial community itself. Thus the integral connection between freedom and community in Paul's thinking again becomes transparently clear, states Banks.26 And it brings special significance in understanding Paul's statement of confidence that "where the Spirit is of the Lord, there is freedom" (2 Cor. 3:17) which contains much of his view of community as already implicit in it. We will see later how this freedom is also a central tenant in Irenaeus' theology of ecclesia.

ii. Reconciliation in Christ: Pauline Communities of Reconciliation

Within the rich selection of Pauline images of the Church, two images are central for Paul, and while one, the Church as the "body of Christ" functions as a basic ecclesial paradigm in Romans (12:1-21), 1 Corinthians (12:1-31), and Ephesians (4:1-16), the corollary Pauline image of members of the Church as agents of reconciliation (Rom. 5:6-11; 2 Cor. 5:16-21; Eph. 2:11-21) prove especially fruitful in our consideration. States Russell:27

> The Pauline households of faith are constructed on a primary foundation of the experience of reconciliation. For Paul, the reconciliatory event in all its power undergirds what it means to be a Christian, to claim Jesus as the messiah. Paul communicates to his households that something astonishing has happened in and through Jesus, and this "something" changes the very nature

of being human. This experience of reconciliation appears as a central and powerful reality throughout the Pauline writings, but it expresses itself most clearly in Romans, Ephesians and 2 Corinthians.

Paul understands reconciliation as a cosmic event that happened on behalf of an alienated and estranged humanity (Rom. 5:6-11). The purpose of this reconciliatory action in Jesus Christ is that mankind might no longer be strangers and enemies of God but friends and disciples (Eph. 2:19-20). This reconciliation in Christ is a tearing down of the "dividing wall" of hostility that separated humans from one another and God (Eph. 2:14); it is an abolition of the law with its commands and ordinances, in order to create "one new humanity in place of the two, thus making peace" (2:15-16).

This new humanity created by Christ, makes the reality and ministry of reconciliation possible. In the Pauline households, anyone who accepts this gift of reconciliation also receives a new power for life, to enter into a new kind of human existence, to become a new creation. But now we have a new responsibility of extending this newness to others through the ministry of reconciliation (2 Cor. 5:16-19).

So there are at least three dimensions then, to this Pauline understanding of reconciliation: it is personal, it is social, and it is communal. To be reconciled in accepting Jesus personally, is to adapt a new perspective about self, life and God. Jesus and the new community become the center around which to organize personal identity and life purpose. As interpreted by Paul, you are a loved and forgiven member of a new family, a new creation. The second dimension focusing on social identity, to be in Christ is to take on a new social-political allegiance. It is to choose to be "over-against" the dominant society, for to be reconciled to God is to proclaim "Jesus as Lord." This process of reconciliation involved disconnecting oneself from the values and mores of the Greco-Roman world; a set of values that enables the creation of a place for the stranger, the exile, the widow, the orphan, and the slave. It was a status that made the Church vulnerable to harassment and attack from political and religious authorities. And the third dimension of the Pauline understanding of reconciliation is communal, the new community of the body of Christ where one was provided the structure (a member of a household of faith) to be nurtured and live out the new Christian social identity in the world. For Paul, it was not possible to experience reconciliation both personal and social without a communal context.

iii. Corporate Maturity of Community—Growth in Faith and Knowledge

Paul's description of the community as a "body" points not only to a creation of harmony between members (which is more the emphasis of his family terminology) but a development towards maturity, generally in contexts of corporate community in view.[28] This maturity is further defined in a number of passages throughout Paul's writings. He views it as an ever-closer approximation to the "likeness" of God, so that there is an increasing reflection of His attitudes and concerns and an increasing participation in His activities (Col. 3:10; Eph. 4:24; 5:1); Christ is also "the image of the invisible God" in whom "all the fullness of God was pleased to dwell" (Col. 1:15,19); Paul can describe Christian maturity as a call to the "imitation" of Christ and as following of His "example"; as a possession of the "mind" of Christ and bearing in one's "person" the marks of Christ; as a "clothing oneself" with Christ, allowing Christ to be "formed" within; and as a transformation into His "glory" (the unique quality that characterized Him); it is essentially an attaining of all to "the knowledge of the Son of God, to mature adulthood, to the measure of the stature of the fullness of Christ" (Eph. 4:13).

How does this transformation and growth take place? And in what way does the Spirit interact with individuals in community to foster maturity? As these were key issues for Irenaeus in his 'rule of faith,' so too the key word for Paul is 'faith,' that allows us to embark upon the Christian life to begin with (Gal. 2;3; Rom. 3;5 et al). For faith is the manifestation of the grace of God, however much human activity is engaged in it. According to Paul faith comes "... through hearing, and hearing comes through the presentation of the message of Christ" (Rom. 19:17; Phil. 1:9; Col. 1:9-10; 3:10). Because the association of faith *and* knowledge (gnosis or truth) is so close here, Paul can even speak of his converts having "learned" Christ (Col. 1:7; Eph. 4:20).

The crucial role played by knowledge comes through in Paul's numerous descriptions of his Apostolic work—that it is essentially the imparting of knowledge or declaring the 'truth' wherever he goes (Gal. 2:5). So it is through faith alone that the process of becoming a Christian begins and it is knowledge about Christ that alone makes it possible.

In sum, it is to "understand" the significance of all that has been "bestowed on them by God," to "not be childish in their understanding but mature" (1 Cor. 2:12; 14:20). But their message is embodied in their *actions* as formulated in words, "not only the gospel of God but also our own selves" (1 Thess. 2:8). Paul can summarize this ongoing Christian life in terms of "faith working through love" (Gal. 5:6). Although for him love surpasses knowledge (1 Cor. 13:8; Eph. 3:19), and knowledge without love leads to self-centered pride rather than self-giving service (1 Cor. 8:1; Eph. 3:19), knowledge alone can introduce one to love and reveal its full dimensions (Eph. 3:18-19).

Paul believes that within the Christian community, the presence of loving relationships between members provides the most conducive environment within which fuller understanding of God—itself a further outworking in love—can be gained. As knowledge occupies a key place in Paul's communities, it makes the danger of false knowledge all the more real, as future Christian leaders like Irenaeus encountered.

As regards the Johannine writings and community, as we stated earlier, they seem to be known for their sharp distinction between the Church and the world. The passage found in John's Gospel dealing with Jesus' so-called 'High Priestly Prayer' (Jn. 17) speaks of the disciples who here represent the entire Church:

> I have given them your word; and the world has hated them because they are not of the world. I do not pray that you would take them out of the world, but that you would keep them from the evil one. They are not of the world, even as I am not from the world. Sanctify them in the truth; your word is truth. As you did send me into the world, so I have sent them into the world. And for their sake I consecrate myself, that they also may be consecrated in truth.

If we try to understand the almost mythical language of John's Gospel, the underlying meaning would seem to indicate that with Christ, something completely new has entered history, something which human society could never produce on its own. Christ is someone absolutely different and new, in whom the holiness and truth of God have become definitively present in the world, a sacred realm of truth. Those who have been sanctified in Christ and live in His truth are therefore sharply distinguished from the rest of society, from its deceit, or institutionalized untruth. And they will be hated by others for exposing it. The moment that Christ and the community of disciples which follows Him lives the truth, the God given construction of reality, the deceit of the world collapses. To the extent that human beings love the truth, they too will come to faith and join the community of disciples. So the Gospel of John would seem to reflect a wide distance between the world and the community of disciples.

iv. *A Johannine notion of Community—Discipleship*

R.A. Culpepper states that the role of the 'disciples' in John's Gospel has escaped the intense interest which has recently been turned on their role in Mark.[29] In John, collectively and individually the disciples are models or representatives with whom readers may identify. They are marked especially by their recognition of Jesus and belief in His claims. Yet, they are not, perfect exemplars of the faith, but of positive responses and typical misunderstandings. They are above all, those who become "children of God." They are 'surrogates' for the Church (Jn. 13:16). And thus it is significant that John uses the term "disciples" (seventy-eight times) much more frequently than "the twelve" (four times) or "the Apostles" (never).

The disciples enter the story when John the Baptist points two of his followers to Jesus (1:35ff). Culpepper observes a typical Johannine conversation that yields to multiple meanings, when Jesus asks the two disciples of John the Baptist a profound existential question, "What are you looking for?" whereby they respond, "Rabbi where do you live?" Jesus eventual answer is to "come and see." C.H. Talbert commenting on this section (Jn. 1:19-2:12), sees a consciously created composition, which focuses on the creation of discipleship and a new community:

> It is significant that the episode 1:19-2:11, which focuses on the picking/ production of a new community, ends the way it does. It ends with the fulfillment of Jesus' prophecy that the disciples will see traffic between heaven and earth localized in his person (1:51) [i.e., Jesus Glorification] ...the spiritual reality that will be dispensed is contrasted with the purification rites of the Jews. Jesus' wine is given at the end of the fulfillment of such rituals and supersedes them. If the episode as a whole is about gathering disciples into a new community, the conclusion is about what Jesus offers them: a religious reality that supersedes traditional Jewish worship. Discipleship leads to a revaluation of Jewish worship in light of what Jesus offers, which is pursued at length in the episodes that follow in John 2:13-12:50.[30]

Philip is the only disciple Jesus explicitly calls (1:43; cf. 21:22). The other disciples who are named begin to follow Jesus because they have been told about Him by another of the disciples. The pattern for the role of the disciples in bringing faith to others is therefore established at the very beginning.[31] The next crucial step is the faith of the disciples which is distinguished between belief in signs and confessions of faith (2:11) as they beheld His Glory. While others may believe the signs, it is only the disciples who have already shown a willingness to "follow" Jesus (1:37,38,40), and remember what Jesus said (2:22). "Abiding" then becomes the true test of discipleship (cf. 8:31).32

We see in the succeeding chapters the crisis comes rather unexpectedly in John 6. The stumbling block is not opposition from Jesus' opponents or demands that His disciples share in the cross bearing, but it is Jesus' words which are the offense. For although they are disciples, many do not believe (6:60). The irony is that while Jesus works attract disciples, His words drive them away. The real test of the disciples is "If you continue in my word [logos], you are truly my disciples" (8:31). The "Twelve" are mentioned for the first time in 6:67 (there is no mention here contrary to the other Gospels, of being appointed or commissioned), as the remnant who survives the collapse of Jesus following (one of whom will still betray Him).

Meanwhile the true disciples continue to share Jesus journey to Jerusalem, whose constant allusions to His suffering, death, discipleship, and life—they do not understand. What is clearer by example when Jesus washes their feet (13:1-20 found only in John), they only understand later (13:7). This story ends with John's account of the last supper at the point at which the Synoptics would lead us to expect the institution of the Lord's Supper, which is not found explicitly in John. Thus according to John 13:6-11, the washing of the feet symbolizes Jesus' saving work, especially His death. Foot washing is clearly meant to be a ministry or service that Jesus performs for His disciples, His Church. The implication which follows in 13:12-17 is that the disciples must accept this work, for the acceptance of this work of Jesus comes to fruition only as they "recapitulate" it on behalf of one another.

At the beginning of the Last Supper we learn that Jesus loved His disciples, who were in the world, to the end (13:1). At the conclusion of the meal He gives them a "new commandment," to love one another as He has loved them (13:34). This disciples' boundless love for one another recapitulating Jesus' love for them, is strongly reiterated: "By this we know love, that He laid down His life for us; and we ought to lay down our lives for the brethren."

Therefore, John understands faith in Jesus as belief in Him that finds specific and concrete manifestation in the disciples' *mode of life*, as belonging to the *essence of faith* (cf. 1 Jn. 4:7-12, 20-21).

In the thrice-repeated reference to the expulsion of those who confess Christ, from the synagogues (Jn. 9:22; 12:42; 16:2), if it points to a historical situation at all as reflecting a period well after the historical ministry of Jesus, nevertheless, points to the Gospel of John seeming to emerge from a dispute over Jesus that led to separation of Church and synagogue. If so, then it is the community itself, which is the kind of by-product of the birth of a distinctly Christian community. However, the real Johannine insight running through the whole Gospel—is that the *doxa* (glory) is seen in the *sarx* (Word made flesh in the world dwelling among us) as lived through transformed discipleship (*diakonia/* service) response to community as an ethic of love.

Whereas there has been a tendency for scholars, says Cullpepper, to see as problematic in the Johannine community the sharp limitation of the ethical imperative to love only the brethren and not the world, it is actually better articulated that what the author of the Gospel (and the Epistles) has—is a concern with relationships within the Church *as* community. For love among the members of the community establishes its unity. This unity, the realization and manifestation of love, is the basis of the community's witness to the truth of Jesus as well as its very existence:

> By this will all know that you are my disciples, if you have love for one another. I do not pray for these only, but also for those who believe in me through their word, that they may all be one; even as you, Father, are in me, and I in you, that they also may be one of us, so that the world may believe that you have sent me (Jn. 13:35; 17:20-21).

Discipleship ministry in John is self-giving service. It is conceived, at least in the first instance as an intramural relationship. Jesus lays down His life for His friends, so they are willing to lay down their lives for each other. Through this ministry of service in love, a positive relation to the world is established, i.e., people may be converted to this reality experience. Washing one another's feet is difficult as a symbol of practical ministry which defines the very life of the Johannine Church as community. This is its subversive insight. The community lives in and for such mutual service. Apart from it there is, effectively, no revelation, no faith, and particularly no ministry and no Church.

In true Johannine fashion, he has forced the essence of the issue of the epitome of Jesus' teaching in this "new commandment." The troubling question becomes do we wish to face it's stark demand or water it down? An even more perturbing question arises, can this reality be sustained seriously over history? Maybe this is the truer origin of the notion of the sectarian nature of Johannine Christianity. The challenge then becomes for 'mission' to come about, that it is an overflow, from the world's observation, of such expressions of love. This redefines the theological quest for Johannine community from the notion of contemporary historical criticism, to more in terms of historical integrity which Irenaeus too would seek to demonstrate.

v. *A Johannine Doctrine of Spirit—A Praxis of Realized Eschatology*

In comparison to the Synoptic Gospels the Spirit might not seem to play as central a role in John's salvation-history. But as Bruce Vawter states, it is by no means correct to say that the Spirit has been subordinated in John's theology.33 What is true is that John has treated the Spirit in a unique way. In doing so, he has brought out, perhaps more consistently than any other N.T. author, the implications of the N.T. revelation that the Spirit of God is more than a personification, but a true person standing in relation to the Father and the Son. In John, the Spirit is presented less as the divine power that has directed Jesus ministry than as the divine power that continues and completes it; the Spirit is, as it were, the perpetuation of Jesus' presence among his followers. Thus, the

Spirit is the principle of the divine sonship that Jesus has made possible for humanity. And John assigns to the Son a greater role in the sending of the Spirit. So Vawter comments that in doing so, John has initiated a more elaborate "triadic" theology, where there are three divine salvific agents with a primarily soteriological function.

The Spirit is the principle of the new life that Christ has come to give (Jn. 3:5-8) and is operative in virtue of Jesus glorification (7:38-39; 1 Jn. 3:24; 4:13). He is sent by the Father in the name of Jesus (14:16,26), which is to say that he is the gift of Christ Himself, sent by Him from the heavenly Father to "abide" with the disciples forever (15:26; 1 Jn. 2:20,27). He is called "the Spirit of truth" in that the life that He gives is a share in the divine existence itself. The life that was revealed in Jesus is perpetuated in and communicated by the Spirit, and in the Spirit humankind's longing for truth is to be satisfied.

This means in practical terms that the Spirit makes possible the God-given knowledge that comes to humans by faith (16:13). In even more practical terms, John like Paul sees the activity of the Spirit manifest in the preaching of the Word by the Church through which the saving power of Christ is brought to humankind. This is the distinctively Johannine designation of the Spirit as the Paraclete in the N.T. (Jn. 14:16,26; 15:26; 16:7. In 1 Jn. 2:1 it refers to Jesus). There is no introduction to the term in the Gospel, so we must determine its meaning from its usage in the passage as—"helper" or "advocate".

Like Jesus is with the Father, upon returning to the Father the "Paraclete's" activity begins and remains till the end of time. The Holy Spirit's activity is to reveal the mind of Christ (16:13) even as Christ revealed the mind of the Father (14:10): "He will not speak on His own authority." But will glorify the Son (16:14), just as the Father has glorified the Son and the Son the Father. In other words, the Spirit stands in the same relation to the Christian of the Johannine Church (and of all times) as that in which Jesus stood to His disciples during His ministry. Thus we are reminded that it is not by the words of the 'historical' Jesus alone that we live, but by the Words of Jesus as made known by the Church enlightened by the Spirit, "He will teach you all the truth" (16:13). In Revelation too, the Lord speaks to the living Church through the Spirit (cf. 2:1,7; 2:8,11; 2:12,17). We see the same emphasis in Irenaeus.

In this context we can understand the particular emphasis of the Johannine realized eschatology as a lived praxis in the Church community. Pervading all, is the presence of the Spirit manifested in Christian life (and whether in worship or sacrament). For John as for Paul the more obvious way in which the Spirit is present—is in such Christian virtues as especially fraternal charity, manifest in Christian community, and in the consciousness of the forgiveness of sins and in the love and fellowship with God (1 Jn.2:3; 3:6,23; 4:8,12-21; 3 Jn.11).

This does not exclude, but neither does it simply mean, the extraordinary manifestations of the Spirit in charismatic activities, which certainly have their part to play in the life of the Church. But life can, after all, best be verified in living actions that can only be divine in origin. Just as Jesus' words and deeds were proof of His origin from the Father, the words and deeds of Christians show forth the presence of the Spirit of the Son (14:27). All the emphasis is not on 'Church order' as on the life of grace lived in the Church rather than on its externals.

This leads to one of the perennial struggles of the development of the Johannine community. Some scholars speculate that because of the Paraclete-centered ecclesiology, it offered no real protection against schismatics, and that ultimately caused the original followers to accept a more 'presbyter-bishop' teaching structure versus teacher-prophets) which became more dominant in the 2nd century mainline tradition, but was as yet quite foreign to the Johannine Tradition.[34] It reflects two aspects: that struggles between Churches are often over a diversity of traditions and the struggle within an individual Church over diverse interpretations; and it reveals too, a familiar pattern of the anguish over authoritative Church offices and the reluctant recognition (as in the Irenaeus communities as well?), of groups committed to freedom under the Spirit—that some form of authority is the only way to protect against extravagant claims or divisive elements in the name of the Spirit—for the Christian communities sake.

vi. The Apocalypse of John—And Communities of Resistance

Regardless of contemporary issues of authorship, of which Irenaeus would *have* accepted, the Apocalypse of John (or the book of Revelation) was written at the close of the first century of the Christian Church, and was addressed to Christians living in Asia Minor in the late nineties (where Irenaeus was said to come from). Its purpose was to help them cope with the difficulty and suffering they were undergoing at the time of emperor Domitian (81-96 C.E.). John's Apocalypse was a response to a crisis of identity experienced by many Christian households in that region. The crisis of identity was caused to be sure, not only by their marginal status as Christians in society, but also by Christianity's separation from Judaism, a process that had been underway for some time.[35]

Faced with growing pressure from the world around them to compromise and conform to the pagan standards of Rome, the Churches of Asia Minor needed help. John writes to assist them in working out an appropriate response. His advice is that the Churches should resist evil with all their might; resistance is the primary mode of existence recommended to these Churches. In fact, it is not too much to say that John challenged these households of faith to adopt communities of resistance as their primary mode of self-understanding.[36] Russel says we can see some of this in the literary genre or style in which John writes—as eschatological, or a future oriented perspective on life lived out in the present. It is to see God as the one who controls the meaning of history and its outcome, even now. So we can respond with endurance and resistance. The Apocalyptic form can be said to fire up the socio-poltical imagination of the poor and oppressed so they can protest and resist with their lives. The New Jerusalem,

God's new city, is offered to the Churches as an alternative vision in the midst of life in "Babylon" or the power of Rome. The Churches, while they live in this oppressive reality, long for and are sustained by the vision of the New Jerusalem. John portrays the New Jerusalem as God's promise to the beleaguered believers that history will not end in tragedy but in 'doxology,' not in defeat but in dramatic restoration and redemption.

This vision was to enable the believer to live not as captive but as witness. The power of the future was to be a source of strength for enduring the power of the Roman Empire. As households of faith wrestled with what it meant to be faithful to God in light of Rome's demands, the image of the New Jerusalem was a vivid picture of God's promise and power. At bottom, John is asking, 'Who's got the power? Whose side are you on?' The task assigned the members of the communities of faith of Asia Minor is to resist and help one another find the courage to stay faithful. The reward for accomplishing the task is in the resistance itself, for those who resist will gain citizenship in the New Jerusalem. "It is done!" writes John, "I am the alpha and the Omega, the beginning and end" (21:16). We need prophetic leadership, implies John, if we are to break out of this tendency to adapt or conform to the world as it is.

Is this also a perspective in Irenaeus to protect ecclesial community as defined in a proactive sense in response to internal and external pressures in the Gaulic society of his day? The question and these various influences will be explored in the next chapter as, 'How did Irenaeus combat inauthentic theologies in his faith communities?'

NOTES

1. I will explain this notion of hermenutical praxis and the key to unlocking Irenaeus theology ("the rule of truth/faith") in the next chapter which will deal with frameworks in which to interpret his implied notion of ecclesial faith community since his focus was on a soteriological christology (and needless to say not in sociological terms).
2. William P. Loewe, "Irenaeus' Soteriology: Transposing the Question" in *Religion and Culture: Essays in Honor of Bernard Lonergan*, ed.'s., T.P. Fallon and P.B. Riley (State University of New York Press: Albany, 1987)pp. 170-171
3. Gerhard Lohfink, *Jesus and Community: The Social Dimension of the Christian Faith* (Fortress Press: Philadelphia, 1984) pp. 31-35
4. Tomas G. Bissonnette, "Comunidades Eclesialess De Base: Some Contemporary Attempts To Build Ecclesial Koinonia" in *The Church on Community*, J.H. Provost (Canon Law Society: Washington, 1984) pp..24-58
5. Lohfink, p. 70
6. J.H. McDonald, *The Crucible of Christian Morality* (Routeledge: London, 1998) pp. 150-179 Influences such as the Hellenistic gymnasium and the ephebeion or youth centres, the genos or kinship family group and benevolent societies (eranoi), or the household (oika) of the Roman domas or extended famila, See also Keith A. Russel who writes *In Search of the Church* (Alban Institute Pub: Bethesda, 1994) p. 3, "The household was the basic organizing structure of the Roman empire, and the Church took the household as its own form for more than four centuries. This factor has gone relatively unexamined by scholars until recently." Russel lists three common characteristics of the N.T. Church communities 1. They were organized around households 2. They were sectarian and 3. they were eschatological in their point of view.
7. Russel pp. 3-4
8. Bissonnette, p. 44
9. Lohfink, pp. 175-148
10. Lohfink, p. 82
11. Cf. Acts 2:42; Rom. 15:26; 2 Cor. 8:4; 9:13; Gal. 2:9; Phil. 2:1; Heb. 13:16; 1 Jn. 1:3,7
12. In the N.T. the place of the reciprocal pronoun *allelon* can occasionally be taken by *heautos or heis ton hena*
13. Lohfink p.106
14. As in Gal. 5:14 "Mutual love" in Rom. 13:8-9 presupposes a clearly defined group and stands in contrast to love "for all" (cf. 1 Thess.3:12)
15. Ibid., pp. 110-113, n 107, 112
16. See "St. Irenaeus of Lyons" in *A Dictionary of Christian Spirituality* ed., G. S. Wakefield (SCM: London, 1993); Robert M. Grant, *Irenaeus of Lyons* (Routeledge: London, 1997) pp. 32-33; 52-53; James G. Purves, "The Spirit and Imago Die: Reviewing the Anthropology of Irenaeus of Lyons" Evangelical Quarterly 68 (Ap. 1996) p. 102; *Encyclopedia of Early Christianity*, ed., E, Ferguson (Garland Pub.: New York, 1990) pp. 472-473: John Lawson, *The Biblical Theology of Saint Irenaeus* (Epworth Press:

London, 1948) pp. 9-10, 159-161
17. Stuart G. Hall, *Doctrine and Practice in the Early Church* (William B. Eerdmans: Michigan, 1991) p. 61
18. Rowan Williams, p. 215
19. R.A.Norris, Jr., "Irenaeus' Use of Paul in His Polemic Against the Gnostics" in *Paul and the Legacies of Paul* ed., W.S.Babcock (Southern Methodist University Press: Dallas, 1990) pp. 79-98
20. Robert Banks, *Paul's Idea of Community: Early House Churches in their Historical Setting* (William B. Eerdmans: Grand Rapid, 1980) p.10
21. Ibid., p. 11
22. J. Ian McDonald, *The Crucible of Christian Morality* (Routeledge: London, 1998), p.25
23. Banks, see chapter 10, 11, 13
24. Rom. 6:3ff; 2 Cor. 5:14ff; Col. 3:3 and 1 Cor.15:20ff; 2 Cor. 4:6,5; Col. 3: 10; Eph. 2:14-15
25. Rom. 6:7,22; 8:10-11; Eph. 2:1-7
26. Banks, p.27
27. Russell, p. 53. Some of the rich images include the Church as a new creation, the first fruits, the new humanity, the fellowship of faith, the people of the way, to name only a few. See Paul S. Minear, *Images of the Church in the New Testament* (Westminster Press: Philadelphia, 1960)
28. 20 1 Cor.1:10; 14:20; 2 Cor. 1:13-14; Col. 1:21-22; 4:12; Eph. 4:11-16; 5:25-27
29. R.A. Culpepper, *Anatomy of the Fourth Gospel: A Study in Literary Design* (Fortress Press: Philadelphia, 1983) p. 115
30. C.H. Talbert, *Reading John* (Crossroad: New York, 1992) pp. 80-92
31. Culpepper, pp. 115-116
32. Ibid., p. 116
33. Bruce Vawter, "John's Doctrine of the Spirit: A Summary of His Eschatology" in *A Companion to John: Readings in Johannine Theology*, ed. Michael Taylor (Alba House: New York, 1977) p. 177
34. See Raymond E. Brown, *The Community of the Beloved Disciple* (Paulist Press: New York, 1979) p. 163
35. Russel pp. 79-92
36. Ibid. p. 81

Chapter 2
NOTIONS OF FAITH AND COMMUNITY IN IRENAEUS

We are speaking here, theologically and historically of looking at Irenaeus ecclesiology, but which must be situated first—within a study of its correlatives in his soteriology and anthropology. This is for several reasons: if we are to understand how Irenaeus thought, we must move in the ways that he thought; he did not deal with specific themes like ecclesiology in a systematic manner but as pastoral situations dictated; and too, that although Irenaeus was one of the first Christian thinkers to deal with theology in a historical mindset[1] he was not sociological or abstract-objectified-minded but pastoral and biblical. So we must tease out implied aspects like his faith communal ecclesiology through his theology and pastoral situations as addressed in his "Rule of Faith/Truth" praxis context. Irenaeus starting point is not anthropology but Christology, and then the Church itself, which becomes the praxis faith community that offers access to the salvation brought by Jesus as the new "Anthropos."

It is to attempt then, to present these insights on community and faith's interaction, from within these dynamics that govern Irenaeus' thought (and make explicit deeper assumptions), which helps shape our method. After a short description of the life and works of Irenaeus, we will look at the two main aspects which define Irenaeus faith lifestyle as his "Rule of Faith" and its relation to his notion of "ecclesial community," (under which are listed his themes of salvation, ministry, authority, the body, Spirit, and liturgy, and so on). What Irenaeus sought to protect was the ecclesial community by defining it in counter-distinction to inauthentic theologies which in turn, defined the identity and integrity of true faith communities.

The Life of Irenaeus

Although very little is known of the life of Irenaeus, he is considered by one scholar the most important controversialist and theologian between the Apostles and the third-century genius Origen.[2] Other Patrologists agree that Irenaeus was one of the first original and creative thinkers of early Christianity.[3] His major extant and most important work, *Examination and Refutation of False Knowledge* (or *Against Heresies*) has survived only because it was translated into Latin by Rufinus whose concern to render it "orthodox," exceeded his desire to render it accurately.[4] Irenaeus is know primarily through his works, none of which is autobiographical. Some personal information can be gathered from fragments of his writings preserved by Eusebius, the fourth century Church historian, who makes it clear that Irenaeus had digested the gospel writer John's theology and the Christian thought prevalent in the Greek speaking East of the Roman Empire.[5] To that material can be added the indirectly personal information any author betrays through factors like style, subject matter, and organization of material.

A Greek by birth, a Roman citizen by circumstance, a Christian by conviction, he was born in Smyrna (Izmir, in what is now Turkey) of Asia Minor. A famous Greek city with a long history (1000 BC) with a devotion to classical learning, including science and medicine. It is there that we learn from Irenaeus the influence of his boyhood hero bishop and martyr Polycarp of Smyrna, who was said to have conversed with John and the Apostles.[6] Later Irenaeus was eager to take part in the mission of the Church and became a missionary among the Celts of Gaul in Lyons. He was possibly sent there to minister to expatriate Asian Christians for it was a common business and social migration route. Roman authorities also settled foreigners there. Sometime later bishop Pothinus and the congregation dispatched him to Rome as a presbyter with a letter[7] to advise bishop Eleutherus about the Montanism schism based on widespread prophetic ecstasy.

While there, in 177, the Christian communities of Lyons and Vienne were subjected to a fierce persecution and Pothinus and fifty other Christians were martyred. Upon his return we find

Irenaeus replacing Pothinus as bishop.8 A letter was written afterward addressed by the Churches of Lyons and Vienne to the Churches of Asia and Phrygia, describing the persecutions recently undergone. It is argued that Irenaeus probably drafted it, as it was written in Greek as were the communities it was addressed to—the Asian communities and to Rome (both Rome and Lyons and Vienne were predominately Greek at the time).9 In it we have a valuable insight into Irenaeus' Christian milieu. It is considered a remarkable Christian community, proud of those members who endured appalling torments, but prepared to acknowledge some had weakened, and what was even more unusual in the early Church, prepared to forgive them. There is little indication of sharp distinctions between clergy and laity (only Pothinus and Sanctus are identified as holding ecclesiastical office). The persecution was in part fueled by a traditional Roman and Gallic pagan piety that resented the Christian foreign influence as mostly Greek Christians who defied emperor's decrees and made converts; and were also exasperated by the German barbarian invasions and emperor rivalry fighting near the city with the resulting faltering economy and security. We hear no more after 197 of the Greek speaking community of Lyons.

Irenaeus was a frequent visitor of Rome. It was the only Apostolic See in the West, in contrast to the numerous Apostolic Sees in the East, and Irenaeus insisted on its importance because it had been founded by Peter and Paul. Demtrios Constantelos mentions that Irenaeus spoke of Rome's *potentior principalitas*, a controversial expression he feels is better designated a "more powerful primacy" than "supreme authority." As well, the term *potentior* is said to be comparative rather than superlative.10 I would agree in that in that context, Irenaeus from the evidence, would seem to have had a rather non-authoritarian disposition except when pressured to protect his community. And that Irenaeus did not recognize a primacy of authority to the Church of Rome is indicated by his intervention in some of bishop Victor's policies. When Victor attempted to excommunicate the Churches of Asia

Minor because of the celebration of the date of Easter question, Irenaeus was the leader of several bishops who protested Victor's policies. He expressed the Greek Churches point of view asking for respect of local traditions which did not affect the essence of the faith. Even though Irenaeus agreed with Victor on the time of observing Easter, he did not desire to see Church unity be broken for those who simply followed other Christian practices.

Back home Irenaeus took over a community ravaged by persecution and torn by internal strife. He tried to find ways to protect the ecclesial community from adversaries such as the Gnostic movement, which actually precipitated, out of a pressing pastoral need, Irenaeus' *Against Heresies* and *The Demonstration of the Apostolic Preaching*. It led to the development of certain principles which secured the unity of the Christian community and became standards in ancient and medieval Christianity. Eleutherius was Bishop of Rome between about 174 and 189, when he was succeeded by Victor who reigned until 198. There is no evidence that Irenaeus lived beyond the reign of Victor, which would have made Irenaeus to be around seventy years of age at that point. He is commemorated as a martyr, but evidence is slight and unconvincing.[11]

The Works of Irenaeus

Irenaeus everyday experience in Gaul and the needs of his faithful there, contributed to Irenaeus moralistic, rather than theological outlook in his ministry. Even his anti-heretical writings were not intended to be a systematic doctrinal exposition of the faith but practical guidelines or what we would call 'praxis faith.' He was greatly concerned with the protection of his flock who faced many erroneous and even exotic theological beliefs.

Irenaeus is considered one of the principal architects of the search for a Christian identity which defined the second century. His work shaped the Scriptures, the exegesis, the theology, the institutions, and the spirituality of nascent Christianity to such an extent that his imprint is discernible two thousand years later, says Denis Minn. He uses the styles and techniques of his day to interpret and write of Christian texts and claim Jewish and Hellenistic writings for Christianity.[12] In spite of his immense importance and contribution, it is surprising to realize his work is little known. One major reason is access to Irenaeus texts are very difficult. Until recently his writings were only available in a stiff, turn of the century English. This has been compounded by serious challenges in understanding his style and content for the contemporary reader. For as Donovan states, the internal organization of the work functions with assumptions alien to modern readers; as well as the content, which engages in confronting second century esoterism and heresy. The seeming absence of a recognizable unity encouraged critics, until recently, to reduce their opinion of *A.H.* (especially chapter IV) as lacking cohesion and coherence, the products of a fuzzy thinker who is well intentioned but inept as an editor. More recently scholars such as Phillipe Bacq have made it apparent that Irenaeus is indeed a systematic thinker, although his system of canons is markedly different from ours.[13]

The Demonstration of the Apostolic Preaching, which was known to Eusebius, survives only in an Armenian translation which was redicovered in 1904 and published for the first time in 1907. It is a short 'manual of essentials' or an apologetic work couched in catechetical form. Although written after *A.H.* to which it refers, it has almost nothing of the polemic tone of the larger work, but after a brief exhortation to the reader to combine bodily holiness with adherence to the true faith (1-2) the *Demonstration* can be divided into two sections: First (3-32) where Irenaeus sets out the central tenets of his 'Rule of Faith,' and the second section (42-97) where Irenaeus seeks to demonstrate the truth of the principal claims of the first part by quotation, interpretation, and application of proof texts from the O.T. prophets to prove the claims of Christ.

Against Heresies (or *Adversus haereses*) consists of two very unequal parts: the first book is the detection, or uncovering of heresy. The overthrowing of these heretical views, which commences with book II itself has two parts. It engages the heresies in Book I and attempts to show their lack of foundation in reason or revelation. The remaining books argue from Scripture against heretical theses. Interestingly, Irenaeus claims at the beginning of *A.H.* not to have studied Rhetoric, or the 'art of words', and to be unaccustomed to literary composition—would seem itself probably, to have a rhetorical origin, as his long, complicated, and carefully balanced sentences makes plain.[14] He hoped to complete his arguments against the heretics in Book III, but by the end he has by no means, he says, exhausted the potential of the Scripture's arsenal against the heretics. With the completion of Book IV, Irenaeus finds that he has almost been dealing exclusively with the parables of Christ. A fifth book is therefore dedicated, which will draw on the straight-forward non-parabolic utterances of Christ, and the letters of Paul, insofar as they have been misinterpreted by the heretics (*A.H.* 4.41.4).

Irenaeus and The Role of 'The Rule of Faith'

What are then, these canons that organizes Irenaeus' thought and action? He recognizes one canon or rule, which he calls the "Rule of Faith" (also called the Rule of Truth) that serves as the interpretive principle of his reading of the Scriptures. He understands the Rule of Faith to be in a dialogical relationship with the Scriptures in such a way that each serves to amplify and correct the other. Irenaeus is the first to use the term "Rule of Faith" which also has a prominent place in his *Proof* (for example, no.3). It was more a form of creedal statement (without being verbally fixed), more complex and different though, than the patterns from the earlier confessions, such as "Jesus is Lord" (Rom. 10:9).[15]

The second century conviction that the "rule of faith" was

believed and taught in the Catholic Church and had been inherited from the Apostles contains more than a germ of truth.
Not only was the content of that rule, in all essentials, foreshadowed by the "pattern teaching"accepted in the apostolic Church,
but its characteristic lineaments and outline found their prototypes in the confessions and creedal summaries contained in the New Testament documents.[16]

Because Irenaeus is convinced that the Scriptures belong to the Christian community in such a way that any valid interpretation must be consistent with the faith of the community, an authoritative interpretation of the faith for him includes authoritative interpretation of the Scriptures. Irenaeus describes the dynamism of the Rule of Faith in the vocabulary of 'tradition,' and thus enters into a discussion of offices within the Church, that invokes the role of authority and other issues. We must see this in the context of his distinctive spirituality what I call his central 'paradigm of Life,' that is marked by an appreciation of the whole of life within the Incarnation and human interaction with the divine (deification); it is a unique appreciation of the spirituality of creation and the interplay between the Spirit of God and the human spirit, which has reflected and influenced primarily Eastern Christianity.

What emerges is a Rule of Faith in an unbroken 'dialogue' between Scripture and tradition, between the letter and the Spirit, and between the Word and the experience of those hearing it.[17] Irenaeus begins the discussion of the Rule of Faith in the middle section of *A.H.* 1(1.10-1.22) treating the various variations of the Gnostic systems, with "the solid truth" (*A.H.* 1.9.5) as he calls the Rule here, and summarizes its content as: under the names of the Three, the one God Father Almighty, who made heaven and earth and all that is in them; the one Christ Jesus Son of God, incarnate for human salvation; and the Holy Spirit, through whom the prophets proclaimed the *oikonomia*, the plan of God for salvation. It is under this third part of the Rule that Irenaeus shows the important role of the Spirit for him, as proclaiming the truth of the birth, life, death and resurrection of Jesus (different from the later Nicene-Constantinopolitan creed, which elaborates this truth of faith in Jesus Christ under the second part). Such is the content of the Rule of Faith, the heart of which is handed on through this dynamic process. The faith belongs to the universal Church, having been proclaimed by the prophets it was received by the Church from the Apostles and their disciples. The Church that accepted the faith guards, preaches, and teaches it, transmitting it as if possessing a single mouth (*A.H.* 1.10). In this way Irenaeus outlines a clear dynamism around the rule of faith which *is* the doctrine of truth, not something different from it. Yet his methodology acknowledges that the truth proclaimed by the Church and its full awareness are limited even by human speech about it. Nevertheless, heretics are those who distort the truth and thus lack the authority and unity in representing the "sound doctrine" of the universal Church.[18] It is important to realize that for Irenaeus, what was at work was not the unbridled exercise of authority, but the *exercise of authority within a believing praxis community* whose norms were in the living faith proclaimed ultimately in the Word and celebrated in sacrament (as baptism and eucharist).

Closely related then, to this 'content *and* dynamism' of the Rule of Faith is its 'function': to *unify the Church* wherever in the world it is found. Because it is what we would call "embodied truth," it is an *ecclesial* tradition that even transcends words or languages used, or the human limitations that seek to impede it. This last point, I believe is often under-appreciated because of our blind-sidedness to the communal dimension of the Church and lack of predominant models as witness to this reality. Thus it is not surprising to find Irenaeus asserting that the Scriptures belong to the Church in such a way that any valid reading must be congruent with the faith of that community (*A.H.* 1. preface, 1). He seeks to describe true authenticity with the analogy of people such as Valentinian Gnostics substituting glass for the emerald of the Word, and mixing the brass of falsehood with the gold of its truth

(*A.H.* 1. Preface, 2).

One of the other assumptions behind Irenaeus's insistence on right interpretation is that what is of prior importance *is* the community's faith in Jesus, and the N.T. which is the written precipitate of that faith and the accompanying transformative gift of the Spirit. This also illustrates Irenaeus importance in formulating a recognizable shape to what constituted the two Testaments. So the Church's Rule determines its reading of the Bible.

In *Against Heresies*, Irenaeus employs the Rule of Faith throughout in various ways, but the whole work is an exercise organized toward exegesis under the Rule. As Bacq points out, for example in *A.H.* 4, there are two literary processes that Irenaeus uses correlatively to structure his thought and both are dependent on the Words of the Lord. The first consists of three Rhetoric steps named: 'announcement' of a Word, 'citation' of it, and 'commentary' on it. This supplies external unity to his work. The second process consists in joining the Words of the Lord to one another, thus supplying internal unity to his developing argument. Used together these two processes supply the formal unity of *A. H.* 4 in this case, and the resultant structure takes the form of "concentric circles" for Bacq, or in fact a "chiastic" structure for Donovan.19

So the Irenaeus' exegesis offers readings steeped in an intimate knowledge of Scripture in the anti-heretic text that allows allusions to carry the weight of an extended linking of his direct quote. It seems geared to an aural understanding, which is not surprising since the low level literacy of his culture would be attuned to verbal rather than written communication. The extended linking of Scripture words allows him to bring a depth and scope of related passages to bear on the theme at hand. Clearly, this second century Christian is a person of intelligent faith, who passionately believes in the Rule of Faith as a guarding principle, and a means to allow the Scriptures to breath life into one another, developing a rich and evocative exegesis for the faith ecclesial community. This has implications for the understanding of Church, the human person and Christian destiny.

Irenaeus and the Role of 'Ecclesial Community'

One of the best ways to summarize the center of Irenaeus's theology is the influence of Paul's doctrine of the "recapitulation of all things in Christ." Human nature in its entirety is assumed by the Word of God, and this profoundly defines and affects Irenaeus notion of "ecclesia," (and the "Rule of Faith" itself too as subsumed within that recapitulation). Christ as the new Adam renews all creation and leads it back to its author through the Incarnation and *then* Redemption. Mary is the new Eve, the mother of all the "living." Human existence finds its exemplar in the humanity of the Incarnate Christ in whom the human race is unified—as exemplified with the ecclesial community. Irenaeus employed the learning of his day (as his own Greco-Roman and Judeo-Christian creative synthesis) but subordinated it to the purposes of the "restoration of all things in Christ." This was done through 'communion' with Christ in the Holy Spirit, where human beings are made incorruptible and through this redemption are made like God. In union with Christ, in the world and humanity—as it is lived in ecclesial community—could the Christian Church fulfill its divine destiny. Let us summarize this in three main categories:[20]

i. *Ecclesiological Significance of the Person—From Biological to Ecclesial Existence*

The goal of salvation for Irenaeus means participation in God, as in His personal existence. It is a personal life realized in God, which should also be realized on the level of human existence. Consequently salvation is identified with the realization of personhood in our humanity. Like Irenaeus, patristic theology considered the person to be an "image and likeness of God."[21]

It is like a comparison of two modes of existence as biologically constituted by conception at birth. A person is inevitably tied in Irenaeus, to a natural disposition or an 'ontology' which can choose not to be subject to the control of freedom, which he calls the 'sin of disobedience'. Thus the persons being can subsists not as 'freedom' but as immaturity. And this selfishness or immaturity of sin causes a second 'consequence' which can be called individualism or separation, which for Irenaeus is the inhibiting of full growth or maturity into wholeness, or lack of 'perfection' and likeness to God. Obedience is an openness to the creative power of God, which is the true glory of humankind (*A.H.* 4.14.1; 16.4). Thus for salvation to become possible, for growth in maturity to happen, it is necessary that the body, mind and spirit be renewed.[22] Our 'beingness' needs to be transformed by a new kind of birth in Christ through the Spirit.

But this new life guided in 'faith,' that is for Irenaeus, a preparedness or obedience to receive from God (and directed by the Rule of Faith or the canon of Truth) is realized in the new ecclesial existence, constituted by the new birth of a person, by baptism[23] (*A.H.* 3.17.1-2). We are talking about a new mode of existence, a regeneration. As Irenaeus says, adapting a Johannine perspective on the cross as the lifting up of the Son of God (Jn. 3:3,7), we too become an authentic person living within a historical reality[24] (*A.H.* 5.1.1; 3.16.6). Jesus realizes in history the very reality of the person. Thus our identification with the person of Christ, in whom we find our freedom in body and spirit.[25] This is lived out and experienced most fully in the Church which is by nature a community of authentic persons in relationship in Christ, as a new participatory *theosis* people. An ecclesial existence thus proves what is valid for God can also be valid for man or woman; freedom is identified with the new being of personhood[26] (*A.H.* 4.37.1).

It is also an adoption of man by God, whose new birth in the Church makes one part of a network of relationships which transcend worldly exclusiveness; so that only in the Church have we the power to express ourselves as 'catholic' persons. (The description of Church as 'catholic' originally meant "general" or "whole" Church; as a result of the struggle with heresies and schisms the term acquired connotations of "orthodox," because the universal Church was contrasted with the more localized heresies and schisms).27 Thus, the Church becomes Christ Himself in human existence, but also every member of the Church becomes Christ and Church, confirmed in our faith life lived according to the Rules' guidance. It is thus a *'praxis' faith community as 'lived' in the truth*. This we acknowledge in the 'doing' of baptism and the living it out as profoundly representative of and summed up in the eucharistic liturgy (the transcendent has enter into history in the Incarnation). 28

Thus, we also see in the eschatological character of the eucharist an ecclesial personhood, in the salvation event.29 It is a dialectic of "already but not yet." The "body" as part of the human person, being liberated from individualism and selfishness in ecclesial existence, becomes a supreme expression of community as ecclesial personhood.

ii. *Truth and Ecclesiology — The Body of Christ, the Spirit and the Eucharist*

We can look at the Christological starting point of our understanding of truth and Irenaeus, or rather we can ask the identification of our concept of truth with Christ — as raising the question of what kind of Christology we have in mind in making this identification. Firstly, we may as many do today with the objectification of truth, or as unbelievers, understand Christ as an individual, seen objectively and historically, presenting Himself for us as the truth. With this way of understanding Christ, the distance so to speak, between Him and us can be bridged by the aid of certain means, which can serve as vehicles for truth to communicate 'itself' to us. Thus, for example, the spoken words of Jesus incorporated within the Scriptures and perhaps tradition, are transmitted, interpreted or even expounded perhaps through a "magisterium", and all assisted and realized under the guidance of the Holy Spirit. And there are those scholars who see Irenaeus this way.

Or secondly, we could with Irenaeus and the Patristic Fathers, envisage a type of Christology in which Christ, as a particular person, cannot be conceived in Himself as an individual. For when we make the assertion that He is truth, we mean His whole personal existence; that is we mean His relationship with His body, the Church, which is ourselves[30] (*A.H.* 4.36.7; 3.19.1; 4.38.4). Here the Spirit is not one who aids us in bridging the distance between Christ and ourselves, but he is in the person of the Trinity who actually realizes in history that which we call the Christ; a relational entity as our Savior.[31] In this sense, our Christology is *essentially* conditioned by Pneumatology, not just in a secondary way as in the first perspective above; we could call this instead a constituted pneumatology. The Spirit in making real the Christ-event in history, makes real at the same time Christ's personal existence as a body or community.[32] Christ does not first exist as truth and then as communion for Irenaeus. He is both at once in His recapitulation of all creation in His redemption. All separation between Christology and ecclesiology vanishes in the Spirit.[33]

Such a pneumatological constituted Christology is biblical according to Irenaeus. In the Scriptures Christ becomes a historical person in initiating His real ministry only in the Spirit (Matt. 1:18-20; Lk. 1:35), which means that Christology's very foundations are laid pneumatologically (*A.H.* 3.21.4). The Spirit does not intervene *a posteriori*, but is the One who gives birth to Christ and to the whole activity of salvation. We can only confess Christ, because of the Spirit (1 Cor. 12:3). And as Irenaeus develops later, for St. Paul the body of Christ is literally composed of the *charismata* of the Spirit (charisma= membership in the body).[34]

To speak of Christ means speaking at the same time of the Father and the Holy Spirit, such is the fullness of the economy of salvation for Irenaeus.[35] In the context of a Christology constructed in this pneumatological manner, truth and communion once more become identical and are meant to be able to be lived out in ecclesiological community as the body of Christ. The truth as seen in Christ and the truth seen as the Spirit are identical, and therefore the Spirit Herself is called "the Spirit of truth" (Jn. 14:17; 15:26; 16:13), only their mode of operation of truth differs. The application of Christ's existence to ours amounts to nothing other than a realization of the community of the ecclesial Church, as it does for Irenaeus.[36] The community itself thus becomes the "canon of truth" in an existential sense, recapitulated into the *eschaton*, as what we would later call sacramental community.

This experience of truth in the Church's existence is realized to its maximum in the course of her historical life, in the eucharist[37] (*A.H.* 3.24.1; 4.26.2; 18.5). This is why for Irenaeus the eucharist is so central to his ecclesial community. The eucharistic community is the Body of Christ *par excellence* simply because it Incarnates and realizes our communion within the very life and communion towards the divine; and in a way that preserves the eschatological character of truth for Irenaeus, while making it an integral part of history and the renewal of the created world of the flesh (as seen in Christ's Incarnation and Redemption).[38] In contrasting Montanism or the Gnostics, Irenaeus sought to make clear that the Word of God does not dwell in the human mind as rational knowledge or in the individual human soul as a mystical experience alone, but as *communion* within a community. It is most important to note that in this way of understanding Christ as truth, Christ Himself becomes revealed as truth not in a community, but *as* a community. So the "canon of truth" as lived out under the "Rule of Faith" is not just something expressed, or heard, a propositional or logical truth; but something which *is*, i.e., an ontological truth — the ecclesial community itself becoming the truth, as is seen in Irenaeus notion of growth into divinity[39] (*A.H..* 4.3.3; 4.20.7) This helps to better situate the notions of authority and Apostolic succession attributed to Irenaeus, more as a by-product of the Body of Christ in the Spirit as the Church, and not some add-on or bulwark against whatever heresy or means to institutional power as safeguard40 (*A.H.* 3.11.11 Harvey). It also means that this kind of truth does not come to us simply as a result of a historical transmission. That is why the eucharistic experience is not the same as history as normally understood; it is conditioned by the *anamnetic* and *epicletic* character of the eucharist which, out of distance and decay, transfigures time into communion and life. Thus history ceases to be a succession of events moving from past to present linearly, but acquires the dimension of the future, which is also the vertical dimension transforming history into charismatic-pentecostal events in the true use of the term. Within history thus pictured, truth does not come to us solely by way of delegation (as Christ-Apostles-bishops, in a linear development), but as a pentecostal event which takes linear history up into a charismatic present-moment.

This illumines a certain understanding of the Church's guarding against all error—for already in Irenaeus, he speaks of bishops-presbyters as possessing a certain *charisma veritatis*, developed from the primitive Church[41] (A.H. 4.26.2). Why? Because it had to pass to the community through communion. The bishop in his function is the Apostle's successor inasmuch as they are the image of Christ within the community: i.e., the primitive Church was unable to see the two aspects (Christ-Apostle) separately. Similar observations could be made about the formulation of truth or 'doctrine' of truth in the Church. If 'truth as communion' is not to be separated from this ontology of the fullness of this divine "life," then dogmas are principally soteriological declarations as they were for Irenaeus.[42] Their object is to free the "icon" or Word of Christ, the truth, from the distortions of certain heresies, especially so as to help the Church community to maintain the correct vision of the Christ-truth and to live in and by this Spirit presence of truth in history. The final intention of all this is to lead to communion with the life of God, to make truth into communion and life.

For Irenaeus everything was to be done to protect the community from distortions of truth, that would endanger the truth's soteriological content and effect the required common eucharistic vision of Christ,[43] to orientate correctly the eucharistic communities. Creedal statements were geared to being truth as pointing to doxological acclamations (of Glory) of the worshipping ecclesial community.[44] And for Irenaeus this truth is not to just concern humanity alone, but have a profound cosmic dimension—for the Christ of the eucharist is revealed as the life and recapitulation of all creation.[45] Finally, we can see a eucharistic concept of truth that shows how truth becomes freedom (Jn. 8:32), in this ontology of the Spirit, the overcoming of divisions is the precise meaning of what Irenaeus called "catholicity" of existence within Christ and His Body, the 'catholic' Church.[46] It is this sort of catholicity of existence which the eucharistic ecclesial community exhibits in its own structures. And the freedom given by the Christ-truth to creation is the freedom to create possibilities (synergy) of 'otherness' within communion.[47]

It is there that the Spirit is simultaneously freedom (2 Cor. 3:17) and communion (1 Cor. 13:13) of love.[48] Humankind is only free within true communion is the Irenaean assumption. Truth liberates by placing beings in communion. Irenaeus challenges us as Christians to learn not to lean on objective "truths" as securities for truth (as others have been want to use him for), but to live in an *epicletic* way, i.e., leaning on the communion-event in which the structure of the ecclesial Church involves them.

iii. Ecclesiological Synthesis Implications—Christ, the Spirit and the Church

Let me now summarize some of the main points I have tried to make by placing what I have said in the light of the actual situation of Irenaeus in his own time and by implication ours. We have attempted to view this as applied to the concrete existence of the Church of Irenaeus and some of the unique and common aspects of his ecclesiology.

Irenaeus theology represents a proper synthesis between Christology and Pneumatology with his "two hands" theology,[49] that is often not necessarily fully worked out nor even appreciated, but has major implications for his ecclesiology.50 The Church as the Body of Christ, which means that she is instituted, as I stated earlier, through the one Christological event—is the Church that is one because Christ is one and owes her one being to this one Christ. If the Spirit is not ontologically constitutive of Christology, this can mean that there is first one Church and then many others. If Pneumatology is made constitutive of both Christology and ecclesiology, as I am trying to show with Irenaeus, then it is not possible to speak in other terms. The Spirit is in this case the one who actually brings about, or constitutes ontologically, the Body of Christ. The one Christ event takes the form of events (plural), which are as primary ontologically as the one Christ event itself.

Thus the local Churches are as primary in Irenaeus' eclesiology as the universal Church51 (*A.H.* 5.24.13). No priority of the universal over the local Church is conceivable in such an ecclesiology. So too, the eucharist by its nature points not in the direction of the priority of the local Church but in that of the *simultaneity* of both local and universal. There is only one eucharist in what came to be known and is implied in Irenaeus earlier theology—the creedal "one, holy, catholic and Apostolic Church." Irenaeus can emphasize thus the unity of the Church where the local or universal dilemma is transcended in the eucharist as safe-guarded in the praxis "Rule of Faith"52 (*A.H.* 1.10.1; 4.35.4).

The important thing about this Irenaean synthesis is that the Spirit must be constitutive of Christology and ecclesiology, i.e., it conditions the very being of Christ and the Church, and this can only happen if two other particular ingredients of Pneumatology are introduced into the ontology of Christ and the Church: namely, eschatology and communion, which again are prominent in Irenaeus but it seems have been very much misunderstood (as evidenced by the later Church embarrassment of *A.H.* 5, and its editing out in subsequent manuscripts).53

If the ecclesial Church is constituted through these two aspects of the Spirit, then all pyramidal notions that have been inordinately foisted onto Irenaeus disappear in a true ecclesiology (or at least the proper function of authority as by-product for the protection of the ecclesial body becomes more evident). The "one" and "many" co-exist as two aspects of the same being. On the universal level this means that the local Churches constitute one Church through a ministry or even an institution which composes simultaneously as *primus* (primary). On the local level, this means that the head of the local Church, the bishop, is conditioned by the existence of his community and the rest of the ministries, particularly the presbyterium. There is no ministry which does not need the other ministries; no ministry possess the fullness, or the plentitude of grace and power without a relationship with other ministries.

Equally, a peumatological conditioning of the being of the Church is important for the opening-up of ecclesial communities to their eschatological perspectives as seems evident in Irenaeus theology and communities.[54] There is the constant tension, which Irenaeus tries to balance as his pastoral mandate to the Church— between too much historicity whether encountered with heresy or even as ascribed to the Church and its traditions, and then those, who suffer from a 'meta-historicism,' that makes them think they are above the material world or think themselves superior spiritually. It is then the liturgical ethos that helps focus, and ground the community in its *raison d'étre* as a eucharistic community. The justification of any true ecclesial Church certainly needs an eschatological perspective; history is not enough.

And finally, if Pneumatology is made constitutive of ecclesiology, the notion of "institution" itself, will be deeply affected. We could say that in a Christological perspective, the Church can be spoken as "instituted" by Christ, but in a Spirit perspective as "con-stitutes." These can make a large difference in ecclesiology. If the Church is presented as "institution" as fact, it is more or less a *fait-accomplit*, and as such is a provocation to our freedom. Whereas, to be "con-stituted" is something that involves us in our very being, something we can accept freely, because we take part in its very emergence. Authority, in the former instance is imposed on us, where in the later case it is something that springs up from amongst us. If the Spirit is assigned a constitutive role in ecclesiology, the institution is affected and the notion of communion must be made to apply to the very ontology of the Ecclesial Church, not in surface aspects only like efficacy or exterior dynamism.

NOTES

1. Demetrios J. Constantelos, "Irenaeus of Lyons and His Central Views on Human Nature" in St. Vladimir's Theological Quarterly vol. 33 no. 6, 1989 p. 352
2. Grant, p. 1
3. Constantelos p. 351
4. Donovan, p. 7
5. Constantelos, p.354
6. Eusebius, Church History V.20.6 This is the gauge for Irenaeus birth (130 or 140 AD) since his boyhood memories had to be before Polycarp is said to have been martyred around 155.
7. According to Denis Minns in *Irenaeus* (George Washington Press: Washington, 1994), it is possible that the Christians of Lyons were conscious that the broader Church was undergoing changes which would lead to a more stratified, hierarchical organization for they seemed aware that status was more important in the Roman Church than their own (Eusebius, Church History V.4.2); and Irenaeus own evaluation in A.H. 4.26.3 of those presbyters whose heart is not in the right place.
8. Minns states that in some Christian communities, the word 'presbyter' and 'bishop' had at least been used interchangeably, and it is possible that Irenaeus himself does not recognize much of a distinction between them. Minns states it needs to be borne in mind that nowhere does Irenaeus lay claim himself to being a bishop. In A.H. V. praef. He tells us that he has been appointed to the 'service of the Word.' See 1Clement 44.4-5.
9. Minns, p. 2
10. Constantelos, p. 357
11. Minns states that the 'martyrdom' is only mentioned once in Jerome's Commentary, and not even in his other references possibly because of a scribal gloss. The next reference is only in the fifth century by Gregory of Tours.
12. Mary Ann Donovan, *One Right Reading? A Guide to Irenaeus* (Liturgical Press: Collegeville, 1997) p. 3. Irenaeus wrote sixteen treatises all of which are lost or only fragments remain as quoted in other early Church writers.
13. Donovon, p. 11. See Philippe Bacq, *De l'ancienne a la nouvelle alliance selon S. Irenee de Lyon* (Cerf: Paris, 1986).
14. Minns, p. 6
15. Ibid., p. 11
16. J.N.D. Kelly, *Early Christian Creeds* (Longman: New York, 1972) p. 29
17. Rowan A. Greer, "The Christian Bible," pp. 107-199 in James L. Kugel and Rowan A. Greer, *Early Biblical Interpretation* LEC no. 3 (Westminster Press: Philadelphia, 1986) p. 157
18. Donovan, p. 12
19. Bacq, "Preliminaire: Structure d'ensemble," pp. 41-47 quoted in Donovan, ibid., p. 16
20. I am indebted to the ideas put forward in John D. Zizioulas, *Being As Communion: Studies in Personhood and the Church* (St. Validimir's Seminary Press: Crestwood, 1997)

21. Alfred Squire, *Asking the Fathers: The Art of Meditation and Prayer* (published jointly by Morehouse-Barlow Co.: Wilton and Paulist Press: New York, 1973), chapter 5 esp., pp. 22-25
22. Denis Minns, *Irenaeus* (Georgetown University Press, Washington, 1994) pp. 62-79
23. Mary Ann Donovan, "Insights on Ministry" TJT no. 1 (Spr 1986): p. 87
24. William P. Lowe, "Irenaeus Soteriology: Transposing the Question," in *Religion and Culture*, T.P. Fallon and P.B. Riley eds. (State University of NY Press: Albany, 1987) p. 171
25. Mary Ann Donovan, "Alive to the Glory of God: A Key insight into St. Irenaeus," TS no. 49 (Je 1988): p.17
26. Constantelos, pp. 358-361
27. Minns, pp. 110-112 (A.H. 3.19.1; 4.25.3). See R.P.Moroziuk, "The Meaning of KATHOLIKOS in the Greek Fathers and Its Implications for Ecclesiology and Ecumenism," Patristic and Byzantine Review 4 (1985) : 90-104.
28. Douglas Farrow, "St. Irenaeus of Lyons: The Church and the World," Pro Ecclesia no.4 (Sum 1995): pp. 346-357 (A.H. 4.18.5; 2.31.2; 5.2.3)
29. Gustaf Wingren, *Man and the Incarnation: A Study of the Biblical Theology of Irenaeus* (Oliver and Boyd: London, 1959) p. 164 (A.H. 3.28.1; 5.8.1)
30. Zizioulas, p. 80
31. Thomas F. Torrance, "The Deposit of the Faith," SJT 36 no.1 (1983): p. 8 (A.H. 5.36.2,3 Harvey)
32. Torrance, "The Trinitarian Foundation and Character of the Faith and of Authority in the Church," in *Theological Dialogue*, ed. T. Torrance (Scottish Academic Press: Edinburgh, 1985) p. 116
33. Farrow, p. 338
34. Cecil M. Robeck, "Irenaeus and Prophetic Gifts," in *Essays on Apostolic Times*, ed. P. Elbert (Hendrickson Pub.: Mass., 1985) p. 111 (A.H. 4.33.6; 3.12.1; 17.2-3; 11.9; 17.2; 2.32.4)
35. Donovan, *Insights*, p.84
36. Ibid., p. 87 (Proof. 3; A.H. 3 pref)
37. Zizioulas, p. 190
38. A.H. 4.20.4; 2.28.6; 5.2.3
39. Squire, p. 23
40. Torrance, *Trinitarian*, p.116
41. Donovan, Ministy, p. 80
42. Donovan, Alive, pp. 284-285
43. Margaret R. Myles, *Fullness of Life: Historical Foundations for a New Asceticism* (Westminster Press: Philadelphia, 1981) p. 30 (A.H. 4.26.2)
44. Gordon W. Lathrop, *Holy People: A Liturgical Ecclesiology* (Fortress Press: Minneapolis. 1999) pp. 14-15
45. Walter H. Wagner, *After the Apostles: Christianity in the Second Century* (Fortress

Press: Minneapolis, 1994) pp. 209-211. See also Wingren, pp. 174-175, 164-167
46. Farrow, p. 334; see also Lathrop, pp. 117, 130
47. Constantelos, p. 360
48. A.H. 4.12.2
49. Wringen, pp. 21-24
50. Farrow, p. 337
51. Roch Kereszty, "The Unity of the Church in the theology Of Irenaeus," SC 4 no.4 (Wint 1984): p. 216
52. Ibid., p. 205
53. Minns, p. 124 (A.H. 5.36.3)
54. Ibid., pp. 125-126

PART II

CONTEMPORARY PERSPECTIVES ON IRENAEUS INCARNATIONAL PARADIGM FOR CHURCH AS FAITH COMMUNITY

Chapter 3

FRAMEWORKS IN WHICH TO INTERPRET IRENAEUS IDEAS OF HOW TO BUILD UP ECCLESIAL FAITH COMMUNITY

Central to early Christian and Irenaeus' thought is the conviction that the Incarnate Jesus Christ is the principle or paradigm (as we would say today) of the interpretation of human experience. Irenaeus Christology is shaped by his theory of 'recapitulation,' which thus accords us with his sequence of dealing with his anthropology and a triple wholistic composition of 'flesh, soul and spirit.' Also, typical of the Church Irenaeus saw himself inheriting, was his notion of the 'place of salvation as the place of the Spirit.' We will see how these ideas are fundamentally defined in the context of Irenaeus notion of 'faith community', as viewed within specifically relevant frameworks to interpret his implied ecclesial community theology. We will see how a 'hermeneutical praxis' can be said to be a sort of 'prolegomena' that defines a key insight into Irenaeus ecclesial communal theology.[1] Namely, Irenaeus "rule of faith/truth" as a statement of a hermenuetics of praxis, and its relation to—a sociological-historical praxis of a community ethos; a 'koinonia' praxis as the biblical norm of a communal ethic; and the praxis ethics of Eastern orthodoxy as ecclesial communion.

As Hermeneutical Praxis— Irenaeus "Rule of Faith/Truth"

The "rule of faith" or "canon of truth"[2] (which is practically synonymous in Irenaeus) is seen by many as a key to interpreting Irenaeus, but usually it is in one of two primary directions with Western theologians or commentators: as a polemic or an apologetic. On the one hand, there are those who see it as a literary device in a polemic defense of the faith like Grant's notion of Irenaeus using Greek rhetoric style and the "rule of faith" as a first *hypothesis*, for Irenaeus to describe his key theological ideas.[3] On the other hand, are authors such a Patrick Hamell who see the "rule of faith" as the true apologetic teaching or 'magisterium' of the present living Roman Church.4 Along similar apologetic lines, is the humanist approach of Hans Kung, who sees the "rule of faith" as operating in a shifting historical paradigm that struggles to makes a person Christian by attempting to live out one's humanity, social life and religion (i.e., our existential relationship to Him) "by the criterion and in the *spirit* of the Christ, [emphasis mine]—for better or worse as is the case with human nature." Kung also says that the rule moved from a "confession of faith" to more a "boundary line criteria" of the "Catholic Church" against heresy as it moved toward a more institutional monarchical episcopal teaching office and chain of apostolic succession and power.5

But I believe the crucial distinction missed by these writers is the more Eastern Christian Irenaean emphasis, as rather on two other aspects, *both* in relationship—of a 'praxis ecclesiology' and Pneumatology. In this context, the fundamental mode most important in interpreting this 'praxis hermeneutic' is the meaning of "the rule of faith" for Irenaeus—but as a key to his generating a "praxis ecclesiology" as "faith community." The following other three modes below in this chapter, can be seen as complimentary or reinforcing the argument of my thesis—of focusing on the vital quality of a 'communal ethic' in Irenaeus as a praxis ecclesiology along with a pastoral theology.

In John Breck's *The Power of the Word: In the Worshipping Church*, we see an Eastern theologian doing a good job in seeking to re-articulate a contemporary response to the modern "hermeneutic problem" with an exploration of the Patristic setting for what he called "theoretic hermeneutics"6 which we will define shortly. Let us see how it relates to a hermeneutic praxis in our interpretation of the role of Irenaeus' "rule of faith." Breck says one of the most pressing needs within the Church today is to recover the patristic vision of the dynamic quality of the Word as the instrument of God's self-disclosure and self-communication. The Word of God expressed in the form of Holy Scripture and traditional creedal formulas possesses an inherent power by which it communicates divine grace and truth.

Within Orthodoxy, the relationship between 'Word and Sacrament' is one of essential unity, where God articulates the economy of Salvation. To Western ears this insistence upon their fundamental unity, may seem strange. For centuries, says Breck, Catholics and Protestants have been enmeshed in controversy over the relevant importance and notion of the two. The West has tended to create a distinction, even a dichotomy, between Word and Sacrament, preaching and liturgy, proclamation and celebration, that is quite foreign to Orthodox theology. In the thought of the Eastern Fathers, grounded as it is in the wholistic nature of the Apostolic vision they are inseparable. Together they form a unique and unified medium of communion between God and humans, a reciprocal participation between divine and human life.

It is vitally important for the continuous and arduous task of bringing *orthopraxis* (true practice) into line with *orthodoxia* (true doctrine). The first step in this ongoing renewal involves overcoming a purely "verbal" understanding of the Word. This experience of the human words being able to become the very Word of God (*kerygma*) is through the inspirational and interpretive *dynamis* or power of the Holy Spirit (Lk. 24:45-49; Acts 1:4-8). Christ's own words are invariable linked with the proclamation of the "good news" of the Kingdom with concrete material signs that reveal the deeper meaning and confirm the truth of His words (Mk. 1:21-27; cf Mt.4:23). So similarly, the Apostolic commission consists in the double imperative to preach and to heal (Lk. 10:8f). This healing—accomplished through the power of the spoken word—is a true "symbol" of salvation in that it enables the restored person to participate immediately in the new creation, the eschatological and cosmic reality of which Christ is 'Author' and 'Head'. That reality is nothing other than the Church: the "new life in the Spirit," says Breck.

This Word of God is primarily communicated—expressed and received—by the ecclesial act of celebration, and in particular of the eucharistic mystery. Without that nourishment, the Word itself loses meaning because it is no longer *actualized* in the experience of the ecclesial community. The Word reveals itself to be a 'Person', the source and sustainer of all that renders truly "personal" those created in His divine image. The Word discloses the mystery of the divine will by creating a deep and genuine "communication," a *koinonia* or communion, between divine and human life.

Breck seeks to remind us how we can apply this understanding to the problem of modern hermeneutics and "higher criticism." One of the problems of modern humanity is that "technological man" is a stunted being, a caricature of the true Adam, devoid of ultimate meaning and transcendent destiny. What is the proper relationship between exegesis and theology? How can we break the so-called "hermeneutic circle" that results from the fact that while we seek to understand a given phenomenon in relation to its historical context, the context itself can only be properly understood on the basis of a prior understanding of the phenomena that determine it? The only way, says Breck to resolve such a conundrum, and answer the multitude of questions that arise from it, is to identify the "hermeneutic bridge" or the link that directly relates the *life-situation* of Christians today with the Word of God as that Word comes to expression in Holy Scripture.

The three major Christian confessions, Protestant, Catholic and Orthodox, have suggested very different answers to the question, "What unites (and thus makes 'relevant') the Apostolic witness to the present life of the Church? Each of these answers appears to have been chiefly influenced by a particular conception of the work of the Holy Spirit within the Christian community. Protestant pneumatology is essentially "charismatic" insofar as it insists upon the spiritual illumination of the individual in their personal reading of the Bible, reacting against the Roman policy of authority domination. The Catholic claim has tended to be that the hermeneutic bridge was assured by the Church through the institution of the magisterium. In the Orthodox Church exegesis is a function of the worshipping Church, because exegesis is properly a theological discipline. The exegete themselves must participate (*theoria = deification = divinization*) in the process of divine revelation.

So in looking at *theoria* as a orthodox hermeneutic:

> A fallacious presupposition underlies this idea that exegesis is essentially a science in the modern sense of the term: the presupposition that history itself enshrines ultimate truth. *Theoria* however, understands the historical event to be an essential *vehicle* of that truth, an earthen vessel that contains an eternal treasure. Yet unlike allegory, it insists that the event is indispensable as the means by which that eternal truth comes to expression. From the point of view of *theoria*, exegesis does indeed investigate the facts of history (including myths and statements of faith as well as persons and events). But it does so with the express aim of uncovering and laying bare the meaning of those events for the spiritual life of the believing community. Stated another way, an authentic *theoria* conceives the aim of biblical interpretation to be the spiritual enlightenment of God's people. The ultimate purpose of exegesis, then, is soteriological rather than scientific; and the exegete is properly a theologian rather than an historian.[7]

It reveals its meaning for us *as members* of the Body of Christ. To Orthodox Christianity this experience becomes actual within the liturgical life of the Church. One passage above all, in the 'Farewell Discourses' of the Gospel of John, relating Jesus' teaching about the work of the Spirit-Paraclete, provides the basis for all Orthodox hermeneutics: "I have yet many things to say to you, but you can not bear them now. When the Spirit of truth comes, He will guide you into all truth...."(Jn. 16:12ff). Thus, to accomplish the task of "hermeneia," the exegete must submit themselves to the guidance of the Spirit of Truth (Jn. 16:13ff). Such a view of the aim and method of exegesis is only possible where Scripture and Church Tradition (through the rule of faith), are understood to be "theandric" or divine-human realities.

Theoria or contemplative vision, then is as essential to the exegete as it was to biblical scholars. The true theologian, as the Fathers remind us, is the person who prays. Recovery of this contemplative aspect of the *theoria* would do much to restore to exegesis its *doxological* quality. For interpretation of the Word of God and the rule of faith is properly a function of the worshipping Church. It can offer its proper place within the believing community, in order to devote itself to proclamation of "all the truth."

As Pamela Bright stated during a lecture at McGill University on "Authority in the Early Church,"[8] it is none other than the intensity of a loving heart grounded in a loving attention as an obedience within the parameters of listening, praying and conversation—it is an authority that is life giving and founded on love and trust. This presupposes community, that is Gospel born and mutually nourished; of a common experience focused on Christ in their midst. Apostolic authority is in the context of the wholeness of truth. Thus, the "rule of faith" of Irenaeus is geared for the whole Gospel and the whole Church.[9]

What I have tried to demonstrate to this point, is that for Irenaeus the very notion of a hermeneutic is how we interpret the 'rule of faith,' as praxis, or lived ecclesial community faith. In this instance, the early Fathers seem to have fully grasped the notion that our understanding of Christianity and of the person of Christ and the Bible is conditioned by *a priori* ideas and commitments which originate in their lived culture (let alone ours!). They made no pretensions about epistemological neutrality or detached objectivity. For them the Church 'community' tradition constituted the only legitimate sphere of Biblical interpretation.[10] We can see, setting aside later alterations and/or distortions of this idea, the original concept of "Apostolic succession," was not so much a succession of ordination, as a succession of living faith and truth as these are embodied in the Scriptures and the ancient 'rule of faith.' So the authority and veracity of the Rule was not established by philosophical debate over first principles, but by the continuity of history in the ecclesial community.

Beyond the notion of the Rule as a source of scriptural first principles, there is the broader and deeper definition, which is often ignored by historians. This I have tried to explore with Breck, that this expanded understanding of the rule and its application nets a higher return on our hermeneutical and exegetical investment. This is the crucial insight of "praxis" as inherent in the Rule's hermeneutic and in its connection to a lived out ecclesial communal ethic. The Rule stands in continuity with the actual faith *and* practice of the Apostolic Church—and as a window in itself to open up Irenaeus theology as generating an implied (or inherent) ecclesiology of community.

When we look at the Rule of Irenaeus through modern eyes, we see a propositional statement and perhaps, a confession of faith at best. While the rule was certainly both of these, it was far more. The Rule embodied the living fabric of the Christian faith together with its doctrine, morality, and liturgy. In other words, what was handed down (*traditio*, from which we derive tradition) was not simply a set of beliefs or ideas, but a *system of life, a praxis, a faith, a transcendent reality*.[11] Viewed from this perspective, the Rule rises out of its two-dimensional role as a simple statement and stands before us as a deep, three-dimensional medium which points beyond itself to the new creation in Jesus Christ. It embraces both the kerygmatic tradition and the living, oral matrix from which the N.T. itself sprang. Reaching back to the Apostolic Church itself, the rule comprehends beliefs and practices that were universally held since the first century.

The Praxis of Eastern Orthodoxy—Living the Faith

John Meyendorff in his "Theosis in the Eastern Christian Tradition" reminds us that in spite of the link of much of Christianity with the rise of Western Christian spiritual traditions, the first millennium of Christian history, its intellectual and spiritual leadership belonged to the Eastern half of Christendom.[12] Later, it was somewhat historically marginalized by a long series of invasions and catastrophes. Nevertheless, its spiritual message has survived these historical trials, and may even help the West today to survive with its traditional values under severe challenge, says Meyendorff.

For our part we wish to explore how this world of the East

shaped Irenaeus theological views and may even be a key to a better understanding, more than we often realize in the West. Irenaeus himself, a Greek who came from Asia Minor, was the last of the great Western Fathers who was both familiar with Asian and Western theological traditions and languages. In his own person he united the major traditions of Christendom from Asia Minor, Syria, Rome, and Gaul.[13] The river Rhone in Gaul carried Christian missionaries from the Churches of Asia Minor to the town of Lyon, a Roman garrison city. These were people grounded in the earliest traditions of the Church. Greek was the language of the Christian communities in Asia Minor to whom the letter of Vienne and Lyon was addressed and probably drafted by Irenaeus (describing the persecution they had recently undergone); as it was most probably also the everyday language of most of the Christians there and Rome at this time, during the first two centuries.[14] In the letter of the martyrs of Vienne and Lyons, only two Latin names occur alongside Greek ones (as the deacon Sanctus is said to have addressed the persecution tribunal in Latin).

Victor the bishop of Rome, who Irenaeus had dealt with over the imposition of the Roman Easter rite on the Asian community rite used their, was probably the first to use Latin (he was a native of Roman Africa); and reflect the transition and dominating importance in the coming century of the Latinization of the Roman western Church (and the cessation of the Greek influence there soon after Irenaeus).[15]

We will focus on four areas where the early Eastern Christian ecclesial perspective is most important in interpreting Irenaeus: 'Deification', the 'Spirit of Truth', the 'One in Three', and the 'Ecclesial Being and Eucharistic Communion.'

i. Deification

Thus, if we are to best understand Irenaeus' thought we must not under-emphasize this Eastern Christian Church influence. The important notion of "deification" or "divinization" (*theosis*) in the famous sentence "God became man [sic] so that man might become God," echoed by many Eastern orthodox thinkers, is derived from Irenaeus reading of scripture.16 It had originated from Neoplatonic religious vocabulary in the Hellenistic world, but was adapted in Christian use and became standard in eastern theology and spirituality as reflected in the Johannine affirmation of the "Word of God became flesh" (Jn. 1:1,14); and of the Pauline notion that the members of His Body are "In Christ Jesus" (1 Cor. 1:29-30); and when in anticipating the eschatological fulfillment God will be "all in all" (1 Cor. 15:28). "Deification" is therefore, a Christocentric and eschatological concept, that reflects the experience of Christ's divinity.17 This is seen expressed in the confession of Peter according to Matthew (Matt. 16:16), or according to John, in the reaction of the soldiers who came to arrest Jesus and saw revealed in a veiled way his divine identity (Jn. 18:5-6).

In Eastern Christian thought and spirituality this divine identity of Jesus is an essentially soteriological dimension of the faith, like Irenaeus. Salvation is an act of divine love, and this love is limitless. Salvation is seen essentially as this passage from death to life, through God the "leader" of salvation (Heb. 2:10), because "He alone has Immortality" (1 Tim. 6:16). Thus God had to become fully a mortal human being in order to make the passage true and authentic, in a way which would be truly ours. But salvation is not only a liberation from death and sin; it is also the restoration of the original human destiny, which consists in the "image of God." Jesus Christ as true Being and Logos (Jn. 1:1), is the living model according to whom every human being was created. He is therefore, perfect human because He is also perfect God. In Him, divinity and humanity—the "likeness and the image" are united in a perfect personal unity ("hypostatic union") and humanity finds its ultimate destiny in communion with God, that is, in "Theosis", or deification.18 This Irenaeus developed in his use of the Pauline doctrine of a "recapitulation of all things in Christ" (Eph. 1:10).

74

ii. The Spirit of Truth

As we see in Irenaeus too, the debates on the divinity of Christ in the early Church show clearly that Christ's identity cannot be fully defined or understood independently of the person of the Spirit, the "other Comforter," whose mysterious presence permeates both the ministry of Jesus and the life of the Christian community. But an accent on the personal is justified in the sense that faith in Christ presupposes a free personal experience, for "Where the Spirit of the Lord is, there is freedom" (1 Cor. 3:17). As a later Byzantium hymn describes it, says Meyendorff, the Spirit also assembles the Church, establishes its order, and accomplishes the sacramental presence of the Body of Christ.

Meyendorff points out that in the Christian East there has always been a spiritual tension or polarity between institutional authority and the ordained ministry, and prophetic ministers (and later the monastic centers), yet it was often also recognized as the *same* Spirit that was invoked on both sides. Conflict could only arise if the 'spirit of error' was mistaken for the 'Spirit of Truth'. Christian responsibility implied by the freedom of all the children of God, required an effort of discernment by all members of the Church who received the Spirit at Baptism (Jn. 2:27).

Meyendorff states that this sense of responsibility by all is not an institutional or legal principle, but an actual spiritual dimension. It does not contradict or reject the hierarchical structure of the Church, but only confronts it with the doctrine of *charismata* (cf. 1 Cor. 12:4-31), all of which ultimately belong to the one Body of the Church, whereas any individual of a charisma can always become unfaithful to it. We can see this in Irenaeus as:

> The spiritual or ecclesial result is that Eastern Christians, while respecting responsible carriers of truth (bishops, primates, councils, etc.), never attribute to them the function of ultimate criteria. This function belongs to the Spirit alone, of which all *charismata* carriers are servants or instruments...This principle of ecclesiology [contrary to Westerners] is one maintained already in

the second century by Irenaeus: "Where the Church is, there is the Spirit of God; and where the Spirit of God is, there is the Church..., but the Spirit is Truth"(*A.H.*3.24.1).[19]

iii. The One and the Three

The Eastern vision of God as both One and Three, has been a vision of living Persons to whom the human being relates, as a person, states Meyendorff. Irenaeus was more concerned himself, with the ways in which Father, Son and Holy Spirit are related to us as the ecclesial community (*A.H.* 4.20.7; 5.18.1), rather than with the ways in which they are related to one another. For the deification or *theosis* of the Greek fathers is an acceptance of human persons within a divine life, which is already of itself a fellowship of love between three co-eternal Persons, welcoming humanity within their mutuality (Jn. 17:21).

The Johannine definition of God as love thus possesses a concrete meaning within what came to be seen as the mutually loving Trinity of Divine Persons, and an expanding meaning of love that includes the whole of creation. (Nevertheless, there was still a need to maintain both the transcendence of divine essence and the reality of communion as distinct but related). For finally, 'God is Trinity' is also model and foundation not only of each person but also of the true human community.

Deification maintains human diversity and pluralism, which fulfills itself not in mutual exclusiveness but in complimentarity and love. That which is authentic in that diversity, remains forever in the communion of God. Therefore, this eternity of human relations established on earth, and thus the integrity of the person, are formally affirmed by tradition, practice, and theology.[20] This remains to today at the heart of Eastern Christian ecclesial spirituality and the importance of its unity, as it was an affinity in Irenaeus.

iv. *Ecclesial Being and Eucharistic Communion*

The Eastern Christian mindset saw the Church not simply as an institution but as a "mode of existence," a way of being. In the first place, the ecclesial being is bound to the very being of God. From the fact that a human being is a member of the Church, they become an "image of God," and it is to take on God's "way of being." It is a way of relationship with the world, with other people and with God, an event of communion. And that is why it cannot be realized as the achievement of an individual, but only as an ecclesial fact.21 Above all this means that the Church must have a right faith, a correct vision with respect to the being of God. Although during the Patristic period, there was scarcely mention of the being of the Church, there was much made of the being of God. God's existence was not questioned, but the 'how' of his existing. Such a question did have direct consequences as much for the Church as for man, since both were considered as "images of God."

Nevertheless, there were still "pastoral theologians" not the "academic theologians", who did focus away from the trap of ontological monism of Greek thought. They approached the being of God more through the experience of ecclesial community or being. Irenaeus above all represented this group (as well as people such as St. Ignatius of Antioch, and St. Athanasius).22 Importantly, in Eastern thought this ontology was primarily represented, and arose out of, the eucharistic experience of the Church. John Zizioulas stresses that while the "*logos* theologians" in the East interest in knowledge and revelation led them in the first three centuries to understand truth primarily in terms of cosmology, the "pastoral bishops" absorption in the life and struggles of their communities led them into an entirely different approach to the idea of truth. As becomes more elaborated in the theology of Irenaeus—the Greek concern with 'being' becomes more evident, yet the response to it remains entirely biblical.

The ontological being of truth is in Christ, the One of "incorruptibility" of being. This was an extremely profound assimilation of the Greek concept of truth as the "nature" of things with the Johannine and Ignatian concept of truth as life. It was the common experience of the Church as community, and especially as a eucharistic community.[23] Sin is seen not as new and evil (as was more so in the post-Augustinian view in the West), but as revealing and actualizing the limitations and potential dangers inherent in 'Creaturehood', if creation is left to itself. What lies behind sin is human beings refusing to refer created being to communion with God. So the eucharistic communion as a community shows by its very existence that the realization of the Church's catholicity in history is the work of the Holy Spirit. But to reveal Christ's whole body in history means to meet the demonic powers of division. Which can only be safeguarded by the pneumatological dimension of calling down upon the gifts of the whole community, a realization of the unity of the Body of Christ.[24]

This centrality and importance Orthodoxy has shown to the attributes of worship in its life and theology, leads it to a "theophanic" and in a sense "meta-historical" view of the Church. It is as a consciousness of its continuity with its Apostolic origins.[25] It is in the context of the *koinonia* community of the Spirit, that can be implied the concrete continuity (tradition *paradosis*) of the Church, so that the *kerygma* teaching of the Apostles can be "continued" in a living way (not just words), in both historical and eschatological terms as a synthesis of these two "in the Spirit." Irenaeus' theology keeps these two aspects: Pneumatology and the centrality of the Eucharist, strongly together to avoid the danger of their separation. As Irenaeus says, the Church is to be found only where the Spirit is, so "Our doctrine agrees with the eucharist, and our eucharist agrees with our doctrine"(*A.H.* 4.18.5). The same could be said of being ordained as the heads of the eucharisitc community, precisely as spokespersons of the living kerygma, as successors of the Apostles of these *communities* of the Spirit.

As Zizioulas concludes, linear historicism, like objectified ontology, becomes instead conditioned by the Spirit in Eastern Christian ecclesial tradition. The *anamnetic* faculty of the eucharistic community involves precisely a living "rememberance" not only of the past, but also the future in the present. These profound insights into Irenaeus theology especially of ecclesial faith community, can only be properly perceived in the West if we take into account and appreciate his Eastern Christian influence, as a balance to the predominance of a Western Christian civilization mindset.

Sociological-Historical Praxis Notions — Of Christian Morality and Community

Relatively recently, scholars have discovered the insights which come with trying to understand the group or the socio-cultural matrix in which we interpret and live our lives in conscious or assumed social contexts.[26] In spite of better understanding of the social or group nature of being human through sociologically informed knowledge of community in the larger generic sense, there is a sense in which 'community' as defined by the original Christian message has not been an option among turn of the century liberal theologians. A time in which, Harnack among the most influential Protestant theologians at the beginning of the twentieth century — could describe as "religious individualism" and "subjectivism" — though he still was convinced, that both concepts also described Jesus' preaching rightly and appropriately! According to Harnack, the reign of God does not come to a community, but ultimately it comes to an individual.[27]

Nevertheless, as Christian leaders and theologians have become increasingly aware of the importance of the social sciences as an influence on contemporary culture and understanding important aspects of human experience, there is generally much less of an awareness of the connections between sociological analysis and ministry itself (particularly in historical terms).
The appearance of Gregory Baum's work *Religion and Alienation*

was considered a significant step in remedying this lack. In it his goal is to "make a theological reading of sociology."[28] That is, sociology can provide us with vital indicators of community in theological analysis. For the Christian the sense of *significance*, the first sociological criterion of community is transformed into the experience of each of us freely attaining our full potential as a person made in the image of God (very apropos to Irenaeus thought). It is "the courage to be oneself" as the personal, as Paul Tillich describes it.[29] The humanity of the part, is intimately bound up with the humanity of the whole. In sociological terms, the second criteria of community is the experience of *solidarity*; from the Christian perspective it is certainly about belonging. But it is much more about holy and whole relationships extended in a social ethic or 'ecumenical' sense of uniting in love of the whole inhabited world.[30]

This social ethic represents the third criterion of community about *depth* of belonging in which human love and friendship spring out of love of God for men and women (1 Jn. 4:19). There will always be tension between the personal and social ethicity as demonstrated in Christian history and theology, but as Werner Stark, after his exhaustive historical investigation of the sociology of religion, concludes: "Our whole investigation...has proved, if it has proved anything, that Christianity has sprung from and remains rooted in, community."[31]

We will now look, at two authors who try to view aspects of Christian life at the time of Irenaeus from a more theological social ethic perspective and its importance in re-shifting our focus on Irenaeus.

i. Ecclesiastical Power and Authority

According to Von Campenhausen the fundamental element to understanding how the presbyteral system, and the accompanying beginnings of officialdom in the Church was achieved, is to look at the concept of 'tradition' and how it came to be embodied and assured in the institution of office. But what he feels is really important, is to see how the affirmation and preservation of tradition are vital concomitants of faith in Christ. That is, "As belief in a particular, historical manifestation and resurrection of the Lord, this faith is throughout bound up with 'testimony', and without the continuance of this testimony in what has always been thought of as 'tradition' it cannot endure." And it is only in the second century, that Christians become aware of this relationship and work out the theological significance of this.[32] The result of their thinking in turn, is the concept of succession, and the belief in the 'Apostolic succession' of bishops. Along the same lines Einar Molland speaks of it in terms of "the chain consists of *witnesses of truth.*"[33] Paul already acknowledges and affirms the concept of tradition, although deriving from a Jewish connotation, the spiritual meaning has been expanded and transformed as derived from a christological sense. He appealed to the older tradition of the resurrection, which he himself received, and then in turn has passed on (1 Cor. 15:1f). As Thomas Torrance puts it,

> We must interpret what the New Testament has to say about 'the faith once delivered to the saints' (Jude 3) which refers to the Body of Christ in the world depended, and which exercised a regulative force in all its witness, preaching and teaching. The Apostolic Church regarded itself as entrusted with a sacred deposit [tradition] enshrined in the Apostolic Foundation of the Church laid by Christ himself and livingly empowered through his indwelling Spirit of Truth, which the Church was bound to guard inviolate in contending for the Faith, and for which it had to render an account before God...In the last analysis 'the Deposit of Faith' is to be understood as the whole living Fact of Christ and his saving Acts in the indivisible unity of his person, Word and Life, as through the Resurrection...within his Church...for he is the incarnate embodiment of the Word and Truth of God in his own personal Being..."[34]

With Irenaeus in the middle of the second century we find a most enlightening account of this tradition of the faith in which he drew out the implications of the Apostolic and Biblical teaching in the context of sustained refutation of Gnostic heresies. Torrance says it is highly significant that Irenaeus operated with a concept of 'embodied truth' or 'embodied doctrine,' for he saw the theological foundation of the Faith and its empirical or historical foundation as identical in the saving revelation and intervention of God fulfilledonce for all in Christ. This meant there was an indivisible reality and wholeness of truth embodied in Jesus Christ that constituted on the one hand, the basis or canon of truth and all efforts to be faithful to the sacred tradition of the Deposit of Faith, and on the other, as the living out or defending of the Gospel. Seen in this context, 'the tradition', 'the *kerygma* of the truth', and 'the canon of truth' were all created as operative equivalents with only differing emphasis. It is in this sense that Irenaeus speaks of the 'canon of truth', for it is only properly the truth itself in its own self-evidencing authority, and only in a secondary sense the regulative formulation of the truth. So we can say that just as Irenaeus operated with a concept of *embodied truth* and *embodied doctrine*, so he operated also with a concept of *embodied authority*, with a ministry with which Christ shared authority in the proclamation of the Gospel, lived out in the witness of service exhibited by Jesus himself as the pastoral care of His Church; as the empowerment of the saving Word that whatever they bound on earth would be bound in heaven, or whatever they loosed on earth would be loosed in heaven.

By its very nature this 'embodied' and 'shared authority' was to be characterized by several essential features:[35] First, the structure of ministry in the Church in its basic character is authentically authoritative in so far as it is geared into and reflects the intrinsic structure of truth and doctrine embodied (lived out) in the Church. This is the real reason why Irenaeus insisted that succession in ministry and succession in the truth are not to be separated from one another. Second, authority of this embodied kind is not transmitted through external moral or judicial relations but only internally through union and communion with Christ, which means that authority in the Church is actuated and exercised in Christ only by way of 'Community' (*koinonia*). And thirdly, it is to appreciate and take into account the transcendent Authority of the sheer

Holiness' or 'Glory' of God, which brought awe to Jesus disciples and put to flight the powers of darkness through the Resurrection of Christ and the outpouring of the Spirit at Pentecost. If we were to summarize our estimation of Irenaeus on the issue of Church authority, it is of a different kind than is traditionally defined. As Von Campehhausen puts it, institutionalist and hierarchical thinking is by nature uncongenial to Irenaeus. This is best seen from his later work *Demonstration of Apostolic Preaching* where all official and ceremonial elements have disappeared, and the idea of succession, indeed clerical hierarchy in general, are no longer even mentioned in his summary of basic Christian doctrine. Irenaeus is more of a Scriptural theologian, for it is only as an extra, or rather only under the pressure of controversy with the false teachers, does he himself in a small number of passages accept the concept of authoritative tradition, in order to show that by this yardstick too, the catholic Church is still superior to its opponents. For *Against Heresies* (*Adversus haereses*) primarily seeks to defend the truth from every possible angle. For the Scriptures are the true treasure of the Church for him.

Irenaeus succession lists lay stress on the fact that what is involved is a genuine chain of 'teaching', not merely a formal, if incontestable series of bishops names (*A.H.3.3.3*), states Von Campenhausen. The episcopal rank of the mediators of the tradition is of no further consequence to him. For in this context as he likes to do in others, he describes presbyter-bishops simply as 'elders' and thus opens up the possibility of including them directly in the category not merely of teaching clerics but of the revered 'Elders' of the Apostolic and sub-Apostolic age.

Thus making clear it is not the teacher of the Gnostics, but the ordinary presbyters who are *found in the Church*, together with the Apostles possess 'the assured gift of the truth'(*A.H.* 4.26.2). By which is meant not some special official 'charisma' but the traditional living doctrine itself. Irenaeus statements on the clergy make it clear that it is not the official position that tips the scales, what matters is the preaching and the life, in the task of caring for the Church, in harmony with one another, expounding the Scriptures rightly—are what must be in keeping with that position(*A.H.* 4.26.5).36

ii. Redefining 1 Clement and the Ecclesiastic Communal Ethic

Among the oldest extant Christian writings outside the New testament, the *First Letter from Clement*—from the Church at Rome to that of Corinth, has long been too, like Irenaeus, used to buttress the concepts of ecclesiastical office, apostolic succession, and the hierarchy of the Church. In a dissertation study Barbara Bowe[37] seeks to critique what she says are exaggerated claims for *1 Clement*. Interestingly, she approaches the analysis of the letters dealing with the conflict in Corinth from recent investigations of early Christian literature from the perspective of epistolary (genre, form and function) and rhetorical theory. They have revealed the extent to which Christian texts were influenced by the epistolary and rhetorical conventions of their day.[38] Looking at Roman rhetorical tradition Bowe sees the letter as a fraternal admonition from one Church to another; and reorients the theology of the whole letter finding Clement had reframed the crisis at Corinth through urgent appeal to 'paraenesis' (moral exhortation) as a communal ethic. Clement challenges the leaders in Corinth that authority is not based in superior spiritual gifts or offices or self-seeking individualism but in praxis of solidarity, service, and communal salvation.

The author's primary purpose, say Bowe, is to preserve harmony in a Chruch threatened by faction. *1 Clement*'s strategy demonstrates a practical ecclesiology which gives serious warning of the harmful effects of the continued discord of individual disputes on communal accord.[39] She sought to assess and describe what would be traditionally termed the ecclesiology of *1 Clement*, namely his understanding and articulation of the nature of the Church and the task of Christian living. One of *1 Clement*'s important images is that defined as the Greek term for brotherhood (of believers) 'adelphotes,' a term which stresses first, as a social group, the corporate nature of the Christian 'partnership'. The group is seen in contrast to those who do not belong to the 'adelphotes'. This 'brotherhood' is dependent on the group's continued efforts to reinforce the familial bonds, especially through ardent prayer (2.4) and behavior toward one another.

From an examination of *1 Clement's* ecclesiological language, several important conclusions can be drawn. First, the 'relational' image Clement employs for the Church highlight in various ways an emphasis on the corporateness of the body of Christians. Christians are described as fellow athletes in a common struggle, as flock, army, household, fellow citizens, and most frequently, as the Elect people of God. These images, says Bowe, and the specific moral exhortations which the images enlist to support, confirm Clement's preoccuption with thecollective and communal nature of the Christian ecclesia, and with the concern for preserving harmony within this group.

> This analysis of ecclesiological language in 1 Clement reveals a dialectical understanding of the church. On the one side is a "vertical"conception of the church which accentuates its order, structure, its proper offices and its call for right ordering of the parts within the whole. The other is a "horizontal" conception which stresses that corporateness and fraternal dimensions of the Christian community, its need for mutual interdependence, and its call for the voluntary disposition of the individual to the common good, wherein the leadership and office are seen primarily in terms of service to the community and obedience is rendered only to God.[40]

Because the crisis in Corinth threatened to fracture, or even destroy the community (both locally and universally), the letter places its greatest emphasis on reinforcing group boundaries, and on maintaining the structures necessary for group cohesion.

Therefore, attention to inner group structures was demanded. They are in the form of *positive* exhortations to attitudes and virtues (specifically submission and humility) which Clement believes indispensable for Christian life, and in particular, for the context of addressing the crisis situation in Corinth as part of a positive Scriptural tradition.41 This includes a careful and concerted effort by the author to strengthen the communal bonds between Christians in Rome and Corinth as fraternal admonition.

The real threat to Christian unity is seen as self-seeking individualism that threatens the very basis of Christian community. And the seriousness of the threat is compounded because, Clement sees the opponents have based their individual claims on superior spiritual gifts. Clement insists that salvation, the goal of the Christian life is not primarily individual, but takes place within the Body of Christ, the Church. Thus, unity and communal cohesion are not a matter of orthodox doctrine but of concrete social praxis. The maintenance of the "harmony of love" (*1 Clem.* 50.5) is of primary importance; so to jeopardize the unity of this social body is, in Clement's mind, the most serious offense. By 'reframing' the dispute as communal fidelity to God, Clement focuses not on the individual rights and wrongs, but on the larger question of the nature of the community itself, and on the need for communal harmony. Individuals within the community, must then subordinate themselves to the good of the whole, and as a witness to the outside society (1 Clem. 54.3).

'Koinonia' Praxis — The 'Communal Ethic' as Biblical Norm

The concept of community *(koinonia)* was highly significant for the early Church. Early Christian literature is unique when compared to that of Judaism in its use of *"koinonia"* community to express an inner relationship between God and humanity.42 Although the relationships involve a mutual giving and taking it is clear that the ultimate ground of Christian koinonia is God's free initiative in communicating or giving Himself. In the O.T. when it does discuss indirectly the notion of communion, it stresses a mutual sharing among Yahweh's chosen people who become a sort of corporate personality. In the N.T. the notion is dramatically deepened.[43] There is a continuity in the basic understanding of human sharing, but what is underlined now is the newness of God's incarnation in Christ. In N.T. terms the understanding of community is encompassed by the word *'koinonia'*.

David Clark gives a good summary of the N.T. notion of koinonia.[44] First, it describes the sharing relationship, or solidarity of God with His people—as Father (1 Jn. 1:3), Son (1 Cor. 1:9), and Holy Spirit (2 Cor.13:14), which has later been conceived as Trinitarian relationship or "holy community of Persons," an ancient theme within Orthodox Christian tradition.[45] Here is revealed the example of the perfect community, wholeness withoutloss of identity of any particular part. Secondly, the word indicates the partnership between Christians in the faith (Phil. 1:5), for koinonia with one another is entailed by our koinonia with God in Christ. Thirdly, the word emphasizes the identity and significance of those in fellowship as unique persons (Gal. 2:9). Fourthly, koinonia is used to describe the mystery of the Eucharist (1 Cor. 10:14ff) where God and His people are drawn together in intimate 'communion.' Finally, the word represents community not only as sharing of relationships but of material goods (Acts 2:42; Rom. 15:26), spelling out the task of reconciling and caring relationships as both the physical and spiritual dimensions of human existence.

Koinonia was one of the many images that Paul struggled with to try to express the mystery of God's love made visible in Jesus Christ. This unique presence of Christ in the believer and the mystery of the Incarnation here find expression. Thus Paul's use of communion may be compared to his image of the body of Christ or to his formulas about Christian living "in Christ" and "with Christ."[46] His usage resembles John's imagery of the vine and branches and John's "reciprocity formulae" about the Christian's being or remaining in Christ and vice versa. The N.T. concept, especially in Paul is closely allied to a concept still very much alive in the theology of the Christian East, as in Irenaeus, about human's gradual divinization in Christ.

It has been recognized, that it would seem that Paul is more interested in the relationship between God and the believer than in the structure of the community, certain scholars feel. In his classical study on *koinonia* in the N.T., Seeseman[47] helpfully sorts out nineteen references and isolates three different categories: communion as participation, communality, and generosity—yet few scholars today would agree with him that the concept throws no light whatsoever on the nature of the Church, says Fahey. What emerges from more recent biblical studies is that communion reflects a double relationship just as charismatic gifts, one enriching the individual and the other forming ecclesial unity.

> The Spirit's presence is not an individual possession to be enjoyed in isolation but is a gift fostering unity within the Body of Christ. Through the Body of Christ the faithful are united to Christ and thereby to one another. Communion in the New Testament implies that Christian's partake in Christ by receiving his Spirit and that they enter at the same time a fellowship with each other in sharing different gifts. Sharing one's possessions through financial support, sometimes referred to as koinonia (2 Cor. 9:13; Rom. 15:26 and Heb. 13:16) is an outward expression of participating in the gift of the Spirit. Paul's reference to sharing in the Body and Blood of Christ in the Eucharist at the Lord's Supper came to be regarded as the special moment in the Church's celebration of its unity.[48]

Interpreted thus, the term community is not as vague. It includes the notion of a voluntary surrender of the individual ends in favor of mutual benefit and support, which is the only possible outworking of the Scriptural injunctions to love one another and not look to one's own good (e.g., Phil. 2:4; 1 Jn. 4:7).

The example of Jesus' Himself provided the model for the "all in common" life, for whatever he had, be it time, abilities, teaching, compassion, or strength, He lavished on others and did not keep it to Himself. As for finances we know that He and the twelve held a ommon purse, entrusted to Judas Iscariot,and that this supply was sometimes supplemented by donations from others (Jn. 12:6; 13:29; Lk. 8:1-3). He proved that the new life which He brought was to be expressed in a new lifestyle, motivated by love. As the N.T. reflects—our heart having been renewed, our life was to speak of unity, justice, honesty, humility, and brotherly and sisterly affection. Both the personal and the communal went together. As the primitive Christian Church at Jerusalem seemed to characterize, it was a community (koinonia) of faith and hope, a union of minds, and the concrete expression of this in the union of goods. It would not have been a community worthy of the name if among the members some lived in abundance while others went in want.[49]

To describe the historical developments of koinonia communion, according to Fahey, from the period spanning the close of the N.T. until the fourth century would be an enormous task. Nevertheless, we can say that at first, there were signs that the basic Johannine and Pauline emphasis would be retained, even expanded. Nowhere is this more the case than in the writings of Irenaeus of Lyons.[50] Unfortunately this bond of unity can be broken. *Koinonia* or *communio* would be eventually over shadowed by other models of Church structure especially as eucharist and Church were divorced in the ecclesiological perspectives of Western theology.[51]

In Irenaeus' *Against Heresies*, he uses *koinonia* some eighty times to describe "access to salvation." In the period closely following that of the N.T., the Apostolic Fathers were particularly concerned about the unity of the Church. In Irenaeus opposition to the false divisions and separations he saw introduced into Christianity by Gnosticism, he appealed to koinonia to describe the communion that exists within God as well as the communion between God and other beings. Koinonia also described for him the communion between time and eternity, even the communion among human beings who share in the Spirit's life. The theological emphasis so noticeable in Irenaeus remains generally short lived. The Church came to focus more and more on the institutional aspects of communion rather than on its source in the Godhead. In this period after Irenaeus, communion was seen, to be sure, as a living relationship between believers and God, but much more stress was placed on the relationship of mutual acceptance between various local Churches. What in itself seemed a shift that was quite legitimate and not undesirable, yet the relationship became externalized by various regulations (as safeguarding formalized community and community teaching) regarding baptism, penetential reconciliation, and eucharistic hospitality. The shifting meant the danger of losing sight of some of the rich complexity of the biblical revelation.[52]

Irenaeus though, could still write that the relationship of koinonia ultimately flows from God's free initiative. Like the Fathers he saw the Church as a 'koinonia' of transcendent origin.[53] In *A.H.*, Irenaeus states that God the Father rewards those "who yearn forfor communion with Him" (*A.H.* 4.40.1). The Father bestows koinonia with Himself to those who have love toward Him. Such koinonia with God is life and light, just as separation from him is death and darkness (4.27.2). The significance of the eucharist as a sign and source too, of unity was soon recognized. On the one hand, it announced the "participation and union" of flesh and Spirit so that when our bodies receive the eucharist, consisting of earthly and heavenly element, we have a hope of the resurrection (4.18.5). And, on the other hand, the eucharist in N.T. Churches meant they could tolerate a great diversity of doctrine and practice while maintaining a corporate unity. But eventually, it was not so obvious how much diversity of belief or practice could exist among the various Churches without the bond of unity being endangered, especially with the presence of rival Churches or leaders.

A test case arose over the celebration of Easter, when the bishop of Rome sought to impose on the Asian Churches the tradition of Roman observance. The different observances had existed and gone unquestioned for decades, until there was a perceived threat to unity when the Arians residing in Rome insisted on following their own traditions. Irenaeus, the 'peacemaker' as his name implies, urged Bishop Victor to pursue a policy of peace. He did not believe it advisable to break ecclesial communion over such a disciplinary matter that was not essential to the faith. It was important to discriminate what was considered to be a real threat to faith and communion.

Though Irenaeus held that certain liturgical divergence did not destroy Christian unity, there were deviations which could not be tolerated. As when he comments on Polycarp's chance meeting of Marcion, that the Apostles and their disciples had such a horror of corrupters of the truth and the unity of the church, that they would not even *verbally communicate* with them (*A.H.* 3.3.4). Those who give rise to schism, "cut in pieces and divide the great and glorious body of Christ", will be judged by God (4.33.7). We can now see from this perspective, how Irenaeus harshest severity or judgment, is only reserved for those who truly are "outside the truth" or "outside the Church" in the context of corrupting and dividing the assembly, the unity of the ecclesial "koinonia"(3.4.3).

In our time, studies such as these on Irenaeus hopefully make it obvious that 'ecclesial koinonia' or 'communion' can be rediscovered as the essential model for structuring the Church in our postmodern society. It is again the task of various Christian Churches to discover how this *koinonia* can with God's grace, become the true norm of the life and structure of unity of the entire Church.

NOTES

1. See Hendrikus Berkhof, *Christian Faith: An Introduction to the Study of the Faith* (William B. Eeerdmans Pub.: Grand Rapids, rev. ed. 1985) pp. 1-52.
2. Joseph Mitros, "The Norm of Faith in the Patristic Age" in vol. IV *Orthodoxy, Heresy, and Schism in Early Christianity*, ed. Everett Ferguson (Garland Pub.: New York, 1993) p. 454-455. Irenaeus was the first to call the preaching of the Apostles or the Gospel "tradition," without implying any contrast between scripture and tradition. He speaks of the faith received from the Apostles and preached everywhere in the Church as "tradition" also (A.H. 1.10.1-2; 3.3.1). A detailed description of canon as tradition (4.53.2) probably developed from the Apostolic kerygma (5.20.1).
3. Robert M. Grant, *Irenaeus of Lyons* (Routledge: London, 1997) pp. 46-49
4. Patrick J. Hamell, *Introduction to Patrology* (The Mercier Press: Cork, 1968) pp. 52-55
5. Hans Kung, *Christianity: Essence, History and Future* (Continuum: New York, 1998) p. 46 interestingly he feels that the Church's three level presbyteral-episcopal Church order (bishop-presbyter-deacon) cannot claim universal validity or be justified absolutely since there was great diversity in the early Church in which this three level Church only evolved slowly in a complex post-apostolic Christianity. This is measured by the intentions of Jesus Himself (mutual service) and the impulses of the first Jewish Christian community (no hierarchy but mutual diakonia) and also the charismatic Pauline community (each has his or her charisma).
6. John Breck, *The Power of the Word: In the Worshipping Church* (St. Vladimir's Seminary Press: Crestwood: 1986) p. 9
7. Ibid., p. 99
8. Pamela Bright, "Authority in the Early Church" (lecture given at Diocesan Anglican Theological College, McGill University, Montreal, Qc., March 2001), Concordia University, Theology Department, Loyola Campus.
9. The fullest early examples of the Rule are found in Irenaeus, A.H. 1.10.1; 3.4.2;4.33.7; 5.20.1
10. Breck, pp. 104-10911. "Dei Verbum," II.8 , Documents of Vatican II, ed. Aaustin P. Flannery (Grand Rapids: Eerdmans, 1984) p. 754
12. John Meyendorff, "Theosis in the Eastern Christian Tradition," in *Christian Spirituality III*, Loius Dupre and Donald E. Saliers eds. (Crossroads; New York:, 1989) p.470
13. Robert M. Grant, *Irenaeus of Lyons* (Routledge: New York, 1997) p. 1
14. Denis Minn, *Irenaeus* (Georgetown University Press: Washington, 19) p. 2
15. George La Piana, "The Roman Church at the End of the Second Century," in vol. IV *Orthodoxy, Heresy, and Schism int he Early Church*, ed. Everett Ferguson (Garland Pub.: New York, 1993) pp. 7, 2016. See Timothy Ware, *The Orthodox Church* (Penguin Books: New York, 1963) pp. 236-242
17. Meyendorff, pp. 470-471
18. Ibid., p. 472
19. Ibid., pp. 475-476
20. Ibid., pp. 475-476
21. John D. Zizioulas, *Being as Communion: Studies in Personhood and the Church* (St. Vladimir's Seminary Press: Crestwood, 1997) p. 15-22
22. Ibid., p. 16-23. 23. Ibid., p. 80
24. Ibid. p. 160
25. Ibid. , p 171

26. See Bernard Lonergan, *Method in Theology* (University of Toronto Press: Toronto, reprint 1994) pp. 115-120, 295-335, who would be one of the first to begin to theologically explore the 'cultural horizon' or matrix that would have us recognize 'in octrine' the expression of the meanings and values that inform Christian praxis, which in the case of Irenaeus, in the Lonergan sense would be first and foremost his mode of expressions as symbolic narrative myth, i.e., the meanings and values of which the validity is patent to faith when faith is viewed with the eyes love, and as the cognitive dimension in the gift and factors of religious conversion.
27. Lohfink, pp. 1-4. In the sense that God could only come to the individual as something profoundly internal and therefore the Church had to be primarily only a spiritual community, breeding an implicit theological individualism whether conscious or unconsciously assumed.
28. Gregory Baum, *Religion and Alienation* (Paulist Press: New York, 1976). See also David Clark, *The Liberation of the Church* (National Centre for Christian Communities and Networks: Birmingham, 1984) who is also a minister and sociologist; J. Ian McDonald, *The Crucible of Christian Morality* (Routledge: London, 1998); Howard C. Lee, *Who Are the People of God: Early Christian Models of Community* (Yale University Press: New Haven, 1995); Gerd Theissen, *Social Reality and the Early Christians: Theology, Ethics, and the World of the New Testament* (Fortress Press: Minneapolis, 1992)
29. Paul Tillich, *The Courage To Be* (FountanaCollins: New York, 1962) pp. 114-151
30. Clark, p. 18
31. W. Stark, "The Sociology of Religion," vol. V in *Types of Religious Culture*, ed. Paul Keegan (Routledge: London, 1972) p. 248
32. Hans von Campenhausen, *Ecclesiastical Authority and Spiritual Power: in the Church of the First Three Centuries* (Stanford University Press: Stanford, 1969) p. 149
33. Einar Molland, "Irenaeus of Lugdunum and the Apostolic Succession," vol. XIII *Church, Morality and Organization in the Early Church in Series Studies In Early Christianity*, ed. E. Ferguson (Garland Pub.: New York, 1993) p. 196
34. Thomas F. Torrance, "The Trinitarian Foundation and Character of Faith and of Authority in the Church" in *Theological Dialogue Between Orthodox and Reformed Churches* ed. T.F. Torrance (Scottish Academic Press: Edinburgh, 1985) pp. 91-117
35. Ibid., pp. 116-117
36. Campenhausen, pp. 169-73
37. Barbara E. Bowe, *A Church in Crisis: Ecclesiology and Paraenesis in Clement of Rome* (Fortress Press: Minneapolis, 1988) p. 438.
38. Mary Ann Donovan in her recent book *One Right Reading: A Guide to Irenaeus* (Liturgical Press: Minnesota, 1997) pp. 10-12 seems to do something similar in using the insights of Phillipe Bacq's studies of rhetorical style in interpreting Irenaeus work in A.H. as the key to his use of the 'rule of faith'.39.
39. Bowe, pp. 4-5
40. Ibid., pp. 104-105.
41. Ibid., pp. 110-118
42. Benard P. Prusak, "Hospitality Extended or Denied: Koinonia Incarnate from Jesus to Augustine," in *The Communion as Church*, ed. James H. Provost (Canon Law Society of America: Washington, 1984) pp. 89-126. See also Micheal A. Fahey, "Ecclesial Community as Communion" pp. 4-23; and John Lynch, "The Limits of Communio in

the Pre-Constantinian Church" pp. 159-198
43. Fahey p. 11
44. David Clark, *The Liberation of the Church* (NCCCN: Birmingham, 1984) p. 11
45. A. Ecclestone, *Yes To God* (Darton, Longmann and Todd: London, 1982) p. 112
46. Fahey, p. 12
47. Heinrich Siesemann, "Der Begriff Koinonia in Neuen Testament," Beiheft Zn Tw 14 (Giessen, 1933) quoted in Fahey, p. 12
48. Ibid., p. 13
49. Lynch, p. 160
50. Ibid., p. 14
51. Prusak, p.123
52. Fahey, p. 14
53. Prusak, p. 110

Chapter 4

FOUR CONTEMPORARY PARADIGMS BASED ON IRENAEUS THEOLOGY AS CENTRAL TO HIS NOTION OF CHURCH AS 'FAITH LIFESTYLE AND COMMUNITY'

We will now examine several modern authors approach to Irenaeus from his 'paradigm of Life, Incarnation, and Deification' and four related sub-paradigm themes we have discerned for contemporary interpretation (namely, creation and cosmos, growth education in divinity, the Body of Christ and the flesh of Selfhood, and the ecumenical unity of Church ecclesia in the orthopraxis theologyof Irenaeus). These are, I believe, fundamental ways of communicatating a dialogical-dialectic context of exploring the ecclesiological tradition of a *community faith* in our times as modern paradigms of Irenaeus' second century unique contribution to Church theology and history.

The Self in the Body of Christ—Selfhood and Community

Heather Ward in her book *The Gift of Self*,[1] reflects on our modern assumptions about the individual, the family and the community in the context of the Bible and the mystical tradition. Her story issues out of her search to make sense of a severe personal depression and a spiritual experience of what she describes as the gift of light from light, a kind of heightened self awareness and sense of personal renewal.

At a certain point, she was introduced to the theology of light within the Orthodox Church, and found in the Fathers of the undivided Church in Irenaeus a vision of personhood which not only made sense of her experience of depression and of light, but also answered many of her questions and struggles about the meaning of selfhood which underlined her journey towards self wort and identity.

Those who have heard of Irenaeus popular dictum ' The Glory

of God is a living person fully alive,' would seem to think it to be in perfect accord with society's current interest in a spirituality of affirmation. But as Ward states, this affirmation of the value of being human is but half the equation for, 'the Glory of a person is the vision of God.' Irenaeus is stressing that the fullness of humanity is only attained when we are totally with God. God, not man must be the measure of human fulfillment. Again, it is a modern corrective to a docetic or humanistic understanding of the self. It is to express the complete nature of humankind. Theologians such as Irenaeus are seen to base their thinking about human selfhood on the account of Creation in Genesis and on the Pauline account of a person as body-soul-spirit.

To become a self is therefore to bring to full expression our spiritual nature, opening it up to God and bringing the psychophysical aspects of our being into harmony with Him. Irenaeus thinks of the self as basically a capacity for receiving and responding to God, not as predominately some pre-existing entity. It is 'through the outpouring of the Spirit' being received by the human spirit that the 'complete' person is made. Our spiritual nature, restored in Christ, is more than physical, mental and emotional attributes derived from nature. We become fully actualized as the self becomes perfected as the human image of God, this reflects the whole being of Man or Woman within their particularized identity, as the Persons of the Trinity encompass the fullness of Godhood within their distinctiveness. Selfhood, then is the capacity for God which is our existence itself, which informs and directs our personality.

'I am because you, God—are' is the self's basic statement of its identity. We cannot make a unilateral declaration of independence from God and from others without distorting, and denying ourselves, says Ward.

> Just as the persons of the Blessed Trinity are distinctive, yet wholly God and truly a unity, we as persons, sum up humankind without losing our uniqueness. Hence it is possible for St. Paul to speak

of each Christian growing to the full stature of Christ (Eph. 4:13) and of our composing the one Body of Christ. As members of that Body we are each our own special image of Christ, playing our part, uniquely in the whole. Together we form a complex, highly differentiated, interdependent organism, not a 'glob' in which each cell is unable to be distinguished from any other.[2]

So when we view ourselves this way the apparent opposition between the private or individual and the communal resolves itself as irrelevant. On the one hand we begin to see that any experience of solitude, of our inner desert, is not for ourselves alone. But that our search for God is a shifting of the focus for all of us that has worldwide significance. For on the other hand, if being closer to God means, we are closer to one another, then once this is grasped, this vision of our communion as persons gives us a new way of looking at the individual-community tension, not only in our liturgy and worship, but it also enables us to articulate a response to social and political issues which proceed directly from this Irenaen doctrine of being human.

Each of us discovers the gift of ourselves as we grow closer to God and each other. This grasp of the primacy of Christian community is long overdue and much to be valued as we see implied in Irenaeus theology. It is here, where communion is a fundamental fact of our existence. We are persons made to know our fullness in the Body of Christ of which we are members. Understood from this angle, we affirm the basic spiritual union as already existent in a Church and acknowledge its various activities as partial reflections of the greater whole.

It also means our acceptance of our poverty as on the way to Christian maturity, like Irenaeus, and provides or enables the Body to function by allowing its continuing openness to life. This provides a powerful counteractive in the Church community. Instead of thinking in terms of talents of the self alone, whether social, physical, psychological, we will also be thinking in terms of self-oblation—of being or giving ourselves within the Body. To live fully our own calling, to live as gift rather than as possessor, is to find our place in the Body, whether it is known by all, or only by God. This vision of community suggests that relationships must be a sign of a wider love, which is the result of our common acceptance of being loved and joined together by God, and of our union of wills with Him.

As Irenaeus tried to demonstrate, says Ward, what is of God endures and upholds through the dynamics of the Spirit. When we look at our own selfhood we see that their is also brokenness and incompleteness. The self seeks its perfection, its 'finishing' in God and is therefore open-ended to Him and others. That is, our community, too, must know the 'broken-open' conditions, its unfinished state. As a human community we do not exist apart from our response to the call of God; our *raison d'etre* is beyond ourselves—a paradox. From this perspective, to experience Irenaeus 'Glory of God' within our ecclesial communities, the circle of community must be broken open to the 'greater Glory' beyond which we are beckoned on to meet. This gives new insight into the eschatological dimension and imagination of Irenaeus.

Too often we think about what ecclesial community is for itself. Yet, of course, just like our personal selfhood in the image of Christ, His Body lives by being given away. We are fulfilled only when we are in fact what we have been made to be: bread, broken and distributed to others, leaven lost in the dough. Jesus too, is seemingly contradictory in calling us 'Come to me, all who are heavily burdened' and 'Go out into the whole world', which is really a balancing out—of our 'sonship' and 'brotherhood' by adoption in Christ, that constitute our very being as Irenaeus would say. For we are working towards the increasing actualization of this reality, a nurturing in our world that rests as our particular responsibility, gifted as we are by the Spirit to discover this fullness to be, is on behalf of others. Like Irenaeus, opposition to whatever distorts or denies this is simply part of our rejection of sin— whether individualistic or collective, social or structural. We are called too, Irenaeus would say, to solutions which recall all to the life of fellowship—as responsive to the Spirit, and as free beings whom God has made free and as equals. Our self identity as a human race, as nations, as 'people', derives not from ourselves but from God, who is for all. It is evident then, from what Ward states, that this contemporary notion of self inspired by Irenaeus, can be seen as well, to be rooted in a faith lifestyle that is integrally related to ecclesial community.

Creation and Cosmos—The Cosmic Christ and Creation Mystics

For Matthew Fox the idea that Irenaeus, an Easterner who came to the West in the second century could say that "God became a human being in order that human beings might become God," echoes the Greek Fathers as creation mystics.[3] We are "partakers in the divine nature," wrote Peter (2 Pet.1:4). So that, the Greek Fathers could also celebrate the divinity of humankind associated along with a lively interest in the cosmos as related to the coming of the Cosmic Christ. A theology of the Cosmic Christ is not embarrassed by the deification of humans. Precisely because this deification is seen in a cosmic and gratuitous context, not as something to fear, but rather one which calls for a joyful response.

But with deification comes a responsibility for creation itself, says Fox. Jesus as the Cosmic Christ was understood by the Fathers as the goal of the cosmos as well as the beginning, the Alpha as well as the Omega. And this thought of Irenaeus, accords a particular importance to the incarnation, which is not just a necessary prelude to the death on a cross, contrary to much of Western soteriology.[4] Rather as representative of Eastern Christian thought, Irenaeus see the incarnation as itself part of Christ's saving activity—conceived as an active obedience to God in identifying with humankind. The incarnation initiates a process which extends throughout Jesus' life whereby he embraces all aspects of human experience except sin.

So that Christ "recapitulates" the sin of the "first Adam" as assuming not only the whole human experience but also the entirety of the created order.

So Irenaeus receives with full seriousness Paul's declaration of God's intent "to unite all things in Him [Christ], things in heaven and things on earth" (Eph. 1:10). Once again as with the early Apologists, a link is forged between Redeemer and Creator. Extending this principle to the Cosmos as a whole, Fox says, Irenaeus envisioned the entire creation radically transformed, perfected by God.[5] Thus, Fox can say, that he believes the issue for the third millennium of Christianity, if the earth is to survive in the next century, is the quest for a Cosmic Christ as a paradigm shift from the Enlightenment fixation on the dualism of a historical Jesus and the Christ of faith. It is a move to rediscover a living cosmology, a living mysticism, an experiential spiritual discipline of insight into creation (as an appreciation of the interplay of science, mysticism and art). It is to awaken the Church and the theological enterprise to this dialectic as its task for our time. For Fox, Christianity, i.e. the Church, calls for a *metanoia of orthopraxis* [emphasis mine]. It will no longer be possible to teach theology with the art of life as meditation, without spiritual disciplines grounded in the body and the arousal of the imagination (or birthing) as integral to learning.[6]

In studying the ancient hymns of the early Church we find that the Cosmic Christ is never presented apart from the crucifixion, apart from the wounds.[7] The Cosmic Christ is pictured as a cosmic lamb slain for all who suffer unjustly. We also learn that the Cosmic Christ is dynamic not a static 'stoic' Christ figure, that is in a sense 'not-yet', still needing to be 'rebirthed.' The Cosmic Christ is, as well, a universal and ecumenical concept. All nations, peoples, and creatures are invited to experience the divine "I am" within them. The Cosmic Christ is not the sole possession of Christians, for Jewish wisdom literature, the prophets, and the apocalyptic writings are steeped in a living cosmology as messianic times will be marked by cosmic awakenings. Apart from the Greek patristic theologians the Cosmic Christ as a vital theme was richly developed in the West through the creation mystics of the Middle Ages (such as Hildegard of Bingen, Francis of Assissi, Thomas

Aquinas, Mechtild of Magdeburg, Meister Eckhart, Dante, Julian of Norwich, Nicholas of Cusa) which happens to represent the last time there was a living cosmology in the West, according to Fox. In naming the Cosmic Christ, Fox lists various characteristics that would have implications for a Christian ecclesiology.

Firstly, the Cosmic Christ and a healthy Church creates *mindfulness.* The Cosmic Christ awakens mindfulness which instructs persons in their need and right to experience the presence of divinity around and through them. It opens their minds and hearts to the universe, to the billions of years and galaxies—of our place in unfinished history of the mystery of the macro/microcosm. It allows a living cosmology to emerge. One way to do this is to take in the wisdom of the scientist as opening new possibilities to the religious believer. New images are born. And lived out. Scientist and religious believer are not in search of different worlds or other universe than what is.

Secondly, the Cosmic Christ is a church which wrestles *with the pattern that connects.* The ancient hymn of the letter to the Colossians 1:15-17 states:

> He is the image of the unseen God and the first-born of all creation, for in him were created all things in heaven and earth: everything visible and everything invisible...Before anything was created, he existed, and *he holds all things in unity* [emphasis mine].

It is the perspective that affirms the scientific quest and the hope on the insistence of an interconnectivity of all things and on the power of the human mind and spirit to a personalizing experience. The crucial connection is made between our moral behavior and our knowledge and love of the universe. It is a statement about the price of being human, that this Jesus had to pay for incarnating the Cosmic Christ. This is something that even the scientist is not exempt from the acting out of the universe. For like Irenaeus, "God wanted all *maturity* to be found in him and all things to be reconciled through him, and for him everything in heaven and everything on earth, when he made peace by his death on the cross" (Col. 1:19-20). For where there is continuity there is discontinuity. But the Cosmic peace that comes by way of the cross makes us realize the paradox of the pattern that in 'dying we find life'. It is the *kenosis* or 'emptying' that is also a part of the Cosmic mindfulness, states Fox. Again the pattern that connects all creatures in the entire universe—emptiness and fullness; suffering and growth.

It is to reconnect belief as the 'pattern that connects'. For all belief is about practice, not just theory. Belief is not belief if it is not launched into *praxis* echoing Irenaeus and the Church Fathers. As the people of God, the Church, we are called to embody our faith the way the lay theologian Clarence Jordan understood belief: "We have come to dissociate belief from faith and we think of belief as a way of thinking when the original intent was not to describe a way of thinking but a way of acting. Actually, our English word *be-lief* comes from the old Anglo-Saxon *be*, which means 'by', and *lief*, which means 'life'. What one lives by is actually her/his belief or her/his by-life. This is the New Testament meaning of belief and faith. It is what you live by, it is the kind of life which you live."[8]

And a vital part of this divine pattern of connectivity includes in a special way the *dispossessed* – those least connected, like the Hebrew term *anawim*, the little and forgotten ones, the oppressed victims of social injustice. As the Moses of old liberated his people, Jesus offered connections to the dispossessed in particular (to lepers, women, slaves, sinners, and outcasts of society) not only by associating with them, but by his own death of disconnectedness and disposition on Golgatha.

This enterprise will require *new wineskins* or *new paradigms* that will, "offer themselves as vessels for the Spirit rising afresh among young in all institutions of church and society; making new connections between world religions, reconnecting our lifestyles to our capacities for creativity, imagination, play, suffering, sexuality, knowledge, and wisdom itself."[9]

Thus, thirdly, the Cosmic Christ redeems us from Chaos, ushering in an era of *coherence*. Whereas the sociologist Robert Bellah describes contemporary Western culture as becoming a "culture of separation,"[10] the Cosmic Christ calls us to end all separations, dualisms, piecemealness—but a cosmos that is always a whole, a unity, a state in the context of coherence. In the Bible the opposite of chaos is always creation--it is the hope that coherence is possible. The "recapitulation" theme of Ephesians and Irenaeus means to "bring together parts which have been scattered and separated." For Fox, this is the meaning of making peace.

Fourthly, the Cosmic Christ as incarnated in Jesus connects the dimension of *space and time*. Whether in terms of science, consciousness, or technology—Jesus is a time and space person, a prophet, an announcer of the new times, the end times (the eschatological), the time of liberation for the captives and sight for the blind, and the time of arrival of the Reign of God in our midst. By uniting time and space the Cosmic Christ challenges twenty-first century Christians and citizens to get in touch with the deep work of the universe. This is also the connection between the *microcosm and the macrocosm* and our inter-relationship to the universe and in the Church as a profound insight that nothing is trivial, that without awe (Irenaeus' 'glory') there is no faith, for the ultimate balance of grounding and marriage is the incarnation story of the human and the divine as Irenaeus would emphasize.

In this dimension of time and space, is also the realization of the Good News of the Cosmic Christ as *Redeemer*—that salvation is about solidarity with God, neighbor, and all of God's creatures. The trivialization of religion comes precisely from the failure to appreciate this solidarity and redemption as a sharing in the suffering and healing of this cosmic redemption. Salvation must be universal in the sense of comprehensive, a healing of all the cosmos' pain, or it is not salvation at all. This we see in the axiom of patristic thinking found in Irenaeus (*A.H.* 5.1.1), and articulated by others, that "not assumed is not healed" as being so important to the Cosmic Christ of Redemption.11

It is finally the realization that the Cosmic Christ is the *revealer of the divine* the "I Am" in every creature. The divine mystery and miracle of existence is "laid bare in the unique existence of each atom, each galaxy, each tree, bird, fish, dog, flower, star, rock, and human" states Fox. It is the fundamental confession for Irenaeus: "We become divine for Christ's sake, since he also for our sakes has become human."12 The divine name from Exodus 3:14, "I Am who I Am," is appropriated by Jesus who shows us how to embrace our own divinity as we are connected with all the cosmos, as created to be in God's image and likeness restored through the Cosmic Christ as a lived reality in our Churches witnessing to our society.

Growth Education in Divinity—And the Future of Humankind

In the book *A World More Human: A Church More Christian*, Conrad Simonson wishes to reflect on the influence of Irenaeus for our times and his unique contribution to the relationship of anthropology to christology.13 Simonson sees him as one of the most interesting Fathers of the Church and one of the first theologians to have a conscious doctrine of being human, and one that was not the norm of his time, yet surprisingly suggestive for our times.

The lure and the dilemma of the Christian faith has always been the man Jesus. There is a fascination and frustration that almost from the very beginning people have talked about Jesus being man and God in the same breath. And even the New Testament documents exhibit in Jesus a variety of ways of intimating both human and divine activity or being. It is not surprising then that the Fathers of the Church did their most extensive and profound wondering about the manner in which Jesus could be said to be divine, which happened at Chalcedon and the Chalcedonian formula speaking of the two natures of the one person Jesus. The problem, states Simonson, is that despite the durability of the formula worked out within the intellectual framework of that time, it no longer represents an understanding of both God and humankind that has an active apologetic usefulness.

Because anthropology and christology are inseparably linked together, whenever the balance between our conceptions of humanity and divinity shift by the dislocaition of one or the other, the christological dilemma presents itself again. That is to say, that both our conception of divinity and our conception of humanity have changed. There has been a shift in the focus on the human and a reappraisal of the role of the divine, as is especially evident in our societal notions of institutional ecclesial Christianity from within and outside of it.

Simonson seeks to set out four aspects of what we might call a growth education in divinity of Irenaeus as helpful for our own time, and the future of humanity.

First, Irenaeus definition of man is *developmental*, not in formal terms. Humankind was the intended aim of God's creative activities, and the cosmos was made for it.[14] Humankind who was not of itself the image and likeness of God, was created in the image and likeness of God by the Son (who was uncreated), in order that even the visible appearance of human beings should reflect their Creator as much as possible. For the Son of God, one of the two "hands" of God for Irenaeus, (the other being the Spirit) was the image and likeness of God, and was Himself the instrument by which God created all things.[15] Here Irenaeus begins to develop a dynamic anthropology, that invests human beings with growth and potential, so that as they grow in their humanity they grow in their divinity.

Taking the "purest and finest of earth" Irenaeus wrote, God mingled his own power with the created stuff of the universe and breathed his own inspiration into human beings. Adam and Eve were "naked and not ashamed" for Irenaeus, because "their thoughts were innocent and childlike." Humankind was created by God as a kind of child who had a long way to go before reaching perfection. Irenaeus did not believe this was simply immaturity, but rather that when created we were not yet what we are latter to become. Yet God placed us on the earth "so that we might have nourishment and grow up in luxury."16

It is so important to Irenaeus theological position that the nature of created things is to grow and develop. Since all created things are in relation to the Uncreated One, and of later date, "so they are infantile." God could not create the perfect being at the beginning, Irenaeus decided, for the Creator is perfect and for that reason all created things are inferior to the one who created them. The imperfection of the created person, even before they sinned, was not the fault of being human, but only a recognition of our natural lack of development. As a boy is not reprehensible for not yet having become a full-grown man, so neither was humankind at creation blameworthy for not yet being what it would later become. As Irenaeus believed growth and development is characteristic of created being, so growth itself, is the continuing creative activity of God.17

Secondly, for Simonson then as a result of Irenaeus developmental view of humanity, the fall into sin is not a fall from perfection, but a *frustration of growth*. In the Garden, humankind still sinned, but as Irenaeus explains it, it was the indiscretion of a little one still undeveloped and easily misled by the deceiver. Man was created to grow in the image and likeness of God, and sin was an arresting of God-given growth. Sin is described by Irenaeus in terms akin to adolescence as the perversion of man's intended development. For sin happening at the early development, meant not only that we would not grow into the image and likeness of God, that is into immortality instead of death, but it would also frustrate our becoming fully human.18

This has had for Irenaeus the effect as well, says Simonson, that since Adam was created to be the lord of creation, his sin had effect on the rest of creation. Earth now brought forth thorns and thistles. As Adam was made of the earth, we are not alien to the earth. Therefore, as there are only two categories of things— created or uncreated, what effects humankind effects the rest of creation. It is just at this point, then, that Irenaeus speaks of the work of Christ who became man, so that through his participation in and redemption of creation, we can see the seriousness with which God identified human beings as an integral part of the created order. It is not a question of the ultimate destiny of humanity as resting in liberation from our essential earthliness, nor that our sin consists of our earthliness—but that humankind's redemption and the redemption of the world are organically one.[19]

Third, as a result for Irenaeus, the incarnation is the resumption and attainment of *true humanity*. In order that the intention of God in creation not be forever abandoned, the Son himself became man to "recapitulate" (the term probably most characteristic of Irenaeus) his own work, and destroy the death that was corrupting the creation. The word suggests something of the recovery of the original, and the bringing of something to completion. The genius of Irenaeus, states Simonson, was to show the potentiality of creation while not subtracting from God's perfection.

Human beings and the world are imperfect, because they are created and not the Creator, yet they still have the potential of 'becoming.' Since we are created beings, and by definition not inherently perfect, we have to grow toward perfection. As sin interrupted our God-given growth, by Christ entering into the human condition we can begin afresh to participate in God's creative activity, where the development stopped and bring our growth to completion.

To turn from the One who gives life and growth is a process of dying. In Christ is the continuation of the work of creation. In a sense, for Irenaeus it is not so much the destiny of human beings to become God, as it is for a human being to become fully human. For Simonson, Irenaeus was trying to make his way between the notion of development on the one side, and restoration on the other. This is the double meaning of recapitulation (or redemption).[20] Fourth, human beings and the world of nature, are so *interrelated* that we cannotbe conceived as apart from history and nature.

Real man, for Irenaeus is a very earthly creature. Humanity was made free, its own master, created to be responsible for everything on earth. Perfect personhood is not a spiritual being, but body, soul, and spirit. So the place of the physical universe too, of physical humankind, is important for Irenaeus understanding human beings and Christ. We cannot be conceived as apart from the created stuff of the world, so that both our sin and our redemption have a great deal to do with the well-being of the world as a physical place. So that recapitulation of human beings was the recapitulation of the whole. [21]

It is by means of the creation itself that the Word reveals God; by means of the world that the Lord is revealed to be the maker of the world. "If the flesh did not attain incorruption," states Irenaeus, "then neither did the Lord renew us with his blood...nor [is] the bread which we break the communion of his body. For the blood can only come from veins and flesh, and whatsoever else makes up the substance of man...And as we are his members, we are also nourished by means of the creation." For this reason can Irenaeus claim that the final result of the work of the Spirit is the salvation of the flesh.[22]

And Fifth, the dogged determination in Irenaeus' theology to talk of humankind, and our future, or our salvation as occurring only in connection with the earth from which we were made, is thoroughly rooted in a *biblical theology*. It defines what is most peculiarly unique to his theology. For instance, the biblical word "recapitulation" as characteristic of his christology is taken from Ephesians 1:10 represents for Irenaeus, an attempt to embody the whole of the biblical proclamation about the work of Christ in a single word. It is the theme of a creation-wide effect of redemption as obviously central to his thought. For whereas the later Church came to see these biblical passages of creation-wide redemption as demonstrated to be possible by seeing in Jesus the eternal, pre-existent One in whom the cosmos came to be, and in whom it exists—today we must see it in terms of Jesus humanity—as explaining the significance of his life and death in seeing his divinity.23

It is not possible today says Simonson, to conceive of humanity without thinking at the same time of our place [as Christians in the Church] in the developing redeemed universe, and of the potentiality of humankind to enhance the world, or ruin it if we loose touch with our redeemed personhood in Christ. The horrible and tantalizing realization, says Simonson, is that " the futures of both humanity and nature as in our own hands, is just now sifting down to the conscious places in our lives. So for us redemption is not something other than creation, but a new possibility that must be a historical reality [something that can be seen in Christ's Body or Church *ecclesia* especially]. It is a view of being human, that says we were created with a purpose, in time, within which being in the image of God, we have reason, freedom, and the moral responsibility to become fully human; but also that we can acknowledge our vulnerability and failure." Then we may see our redemption as what Irenaeus suggested, as a new possibility to realize our own full and mature humanity.24

The Ecumenical Unity of the Church—Ecclesial Orthopraxis

A central concern in Irenaeus's theology according, to theologian Roch Kereszty, is the aspect of 'unity', in its various forms and applications.25 He believes it is only partly explicable by Irenaeus' anti-Gnostic polemics, but more fundamentally related to a dynamism of faith and its resultant theology and concept of church. It was the revelation of the only one God, through the Son Jesus Christ. God was revealing himself through his Word from the beginning of history, thus preparing the coming of his Word in the flesh as Jesus Christ the truly One—as both a God and Man. So contrary to the anti-flesh thrust of Gnostic thought, Irenaeus stressed that the Word became flesh so that he might communicate his Spirit to our flesh. Yet the thrust is a progressive transformation by the Spirit into the likeness of the Son, as the beginning and the end (the first Adam redeemed by the second) so that our humanity will be admitted to personal communion with the Father and be filled with his life (the full recapitulation through the Spirit in the Son).

i. Ecclesial Unity—Forms and Structures

So where does the concept of Church fit into this Irenaean praxis synthesis? He uses the term 'ecclesia' only for the central phase of salvation history, i.e., the community in and through which the Spirit communicates.26 Christ is to all humankind and transforms humankind into the Body of Christ. The Old Testament prepares for the Church, the people of Israel anticipate it, and the Churchitself is the beginning and anticipation of the final consummation, the heavenly Jerusalem. 'Ecclesia' in Irenaeus often appears in the singular, meaning the universal Church scattered all over the world to its farthest ends. He also uses the same term of the Church in a given place (e.g., "the Church in Rome" or "the Church in Smyrna"). By using the same term about universal Church without any further modifications, he indicates that he considers these two things in some sense identical. In other words, the local Church is the Church at a given place, but only in communion with all the local Churches.27

Irenaeus knew from personal experience the Church of Asia Minor, Rome and Gaul, as well as the heretical manifestations of his time. Thus when he speaks about the unity of the "Churches everywhere," or of "the Church throughout the whole world" it is with the conviction of personal experience. For Irenaeus, unity is such a distinctive mark (and that sets it apart from heresies), that it reveals something so essential to and in the Church, that we cannot speak about the Church without also elaborating on its unity. "The same shape of Church order" [appears in] "the ancient structure of the Church throughout the whole world" (*A.H.* 5.33.8; 4.33.8). There appears an even more fundamental unity than the same Church order everywhere in the world, in that it is presented by Irenaeus as in a way, one subject of action:

> She...believes these points [the faith received from the Apostles] just as if she had but one soul, and one and the same heart, and she proclaims them, and teaches them, and hands them down, with perfect harmony, as if she possesses only one mouth. For although the languages of the world are dissimilar, yet the import of the tradition is one and the same. For the Churches which have been planted in Germany do not believe or hand down anything different, nor do those in Spain, nor those in Gaul, nor those in the East, nor those in Egypt, nor those in Lybia, nor those which have been established in the central regions of the world, so also the preaching of the truth shines everywhere, and enlightens all men [sic] that are willing to come to a knowledge of the truth.(*A.H.*1.10.2)

Not only does the Church appear as one agent in preserving and proclaiming the faith she has received, says Kereszty of St. Irenaeus, but it is one subject in offering a pure sacrifice to God offered throughout the world.28 The Church is also viewed as one under the image of a mother as those who separate themselves from the Church are not nourished to life by her breasts (*A.H.* 24.1; 3.25.7; *Demo.* 94).

This unity of the Church extends to not only the Church acting as one subject in process, but implies also the same object of faith. Expressions such as "one and the same faith," "one and the same doctrine," "one and the same way of salvation" are interchangeable and synonymous in their reference to unity. Everyone in the Church believes in one and the same God the Father, in one and the same plan of salvation leading to the incarnation of the Son of God; and everyone acknowledges the same gift of the Spirit, expects the same coming of the Lord, and waits for the same salvation of the whole person, body and soul (*A.H.* 5. 20.1). This does not mean the one and same faith is reduced to a verbally fixed formula, creed or set of propositions definitively and exhaustively summarized. It is more, on the one hand a basic display of conceptual unity, and on the other hand, a reflection of a deeper convergence of a variety of formulations of what the Christian faith or "the rule of truth" entails in the *life* of the believer. that is, that the oneness of faith transcends any rigidly fixed formula, but reflects the important emphasis of the *faith* in addressing various praxis ecclesial contexts like combating the Gnostic heresies (*A.H.* 1.10.2).29 Here for Irenaeus, not even the power, or deficiency— of speech--by Church leaders can amplify or diminish these truths of the faith, when they are in unity with the "Master." One is not afraid either, to explore further the mysteries of the faith, yet in the final act, it is not the act of knowing (as in Gnostic speculation) the truth, but of praise for God's unsearchable wisdom and impenetrable mystery.30

Another distinctive praxis mark for the Church of Irenaeus as interrelated with the unity of faith, states Kereszty, is its *unity in morals*. As members of the ecclesia, all are keepers of the precepts, given by the Word as already in the Old Testament and fulfilled and extended in Christ. They have as their goal the establishing of friendship between God and Humankind, which is based on justice and generosity of love among all. It is particularly a 'morality of freedom' in Christian community. Just as a freed person has more devotion to his master than the slave, so has the Christian for God. It means an abstaining now, not only from evil acts, but also unhealthy words and desires (*A.H.* 4.13.1-2). Put in positive terms, we have love and fear (awe) of God as our Father (*A.H.* 16.4).

ii. *Apostolic Unity—The Contemporary and Apostolic Church*

As we have just spoken of the unity of the Church extended in space throughout the whole world, it is also inseparably linked to the unity extended in time. Unity of the Church in space are correlative. The unity of the Churches scattered throughout the world presupposes an identity with their beginnings. In other words, the present Church is the same everywhere because she is everywhere identical with the Church of the Apostles. And for Irenaeus this was contrary to the heretics (*A.H.* 3.12.7).

According to Irenaeus, the Apostles founded the Church (*A.H.* 3.3.1; 3.3.3; 3.3.4) in terms of laying down the foundations in two ways: they handed over the faith or doctrine, but also the Church *itself*. Part of this handing over "the Church at every place" was to pass it on to bishops (although the term seems to have been used interchangeably with presbyters or wise elders by Irenaeus in a less formal way, still reflecting a regional diversity at this point in time).[31]

So the Apostles passed on this full notion of the Church itself as containing all those elements which fundamentally make up the Church. This is why, says Kereszty, that Irenaeus believed at his time, not only the doctrines of the Apostles, but also "the original structure of the Church" existed everywhere in the world.[32]

The essential elements Irenaeus believed that assured the identity of the Church of his day with that of the Apostles included besides Apostolic preaching and the sacraments of Baptism and the Eucharist, also very important to him—was the continuance of charisms. It seems that like the Church of the Apostles times, the Church of Irenaeus also displayed an abundance of charisms, such as speaking in all languages (tongues or *glossalea*), revealing the secrets of people for their benefit (a kind of clairvoyance), explaining the mysteries of God (prophecy *A.H.* 5.6.1), healing the lame and blind, and even raising the dead to life (2.31.1). The most important charism for Irenaeus is the gift of love as present in the Church from the beginning. It is interesting to view the role this last charism must have played in the martyrs of Lyons and Vienne for Irenaeus. For it

> ...is more precious than knowledge, more glorious than prophecy, and excels all other gifts. Wherefore the Church does in every place, because of that love which she cherishes towards God, send forward, throughout all time, a multitude of martyrs to the Father (*A.H.* 33.8-9)

Here again is the Irenaean unity notion of the 'one subject in process', where the love of God and the displaying of this love in the multitude of martyrs is throughout the ages and everywhere in the world. Implicit in the love charism and also of vital importance as a guarantee against any distortion, is the Apostolic charism of truth, which is actually the teaching mission which the Apostles handed over. Irenaeus develops this as his 'rule of truth' as fundamental (as I stated earlier) to his hermeneutic of ecclesial orthopraxis (*A.H.*3.1; 5.26.5).33

From another perspective Irenaeus develops this notion of truth in the four Gospels themselves as supporting the Church throughout the ages. The Church leaders do not teach something other than what is found in the Scriptures, but rather explain and confirm it. The "fourfold Gospel [is] bound together by the one Spirit"34 (*A.H.* 3.11.8; cf. also 3.1.1). That Irenaeus accepts all four Gospels as the 'columns' on which the Church is built (3.11.8) shows clearly the breath of his vision of unity. As Kereszty states, he is the first Church Father who clearly sees as making use of all four Gospels that originated and were used first in *different milieus* of the early church.35 He consciously accepts their divergencies, rather than opting for one version against other. This broad "ecumenical" basis of Irenaeus's Christianity is in sharp contrast to other Gnostic writers such as Marcion's canon of sacred books, whose selective and exclusive use of Scripture divides them, and the oneness or unity of the faith communities as well.

iii. *The Biblical Unity of the Two Testaments—Two Peoples*

Although Irenaeus uses the Greek term *ecclesia* only for the people of the New Covenant leading up to the final consummation in the heavenly Jerusalem, the whole of humankind, from the beginning of history is related to the Church. Irenaeus develops a particularly close link in reference to the Israel of the Old Testament and the Church. Their unity and sameness are expressed by terms such as "Prophets and Apostles," "the older and the younger people," and "the two assemblies" (*synagogae*). Yet where there are differences between the two peoples, they are contrasted as "the People" and "the Church" (*A.H.* 4.27.5). Irenaeus calls the prophets "the members of Christ" insofar as each shows in himself or their prophecies some aspect of Christ and aspect of His work. Taken as a whole, they sketch out in advance (*praefiguratio, praeformantes*) the *whole* Christ and *all* His work (*A.H.* 4.33.10). This is considered to be done so completely, that if one compares the Gospel given by the Apostles and the Prophets "you will find the whole activity, the whole doctrine, and the whole passion of our Lord predicted in them" (4.34.1). And just so as Christ is prefigured in the Prophets, so is the Church:

> ...just as in the first (economy of God) we were prefigured and announced beforehand, so do they [the Patriarchs and the Prophets] receive their perfect form in us, that is, in the Church and receive the reward for their labors (*A.H.* 2.22.2)

So both peoples issued from Abraham, but only the Church as the object of God's promises, is His true seed (4.7.1; 4.8.1). Although Abraham is not only a Prophet for the Church, but also the father of all who believe (4.20.12). In contrasting the two peoples, as the older and younger one, they are prefigured by Esau and Jacob (4.21.2), in Phares and Zara of Thamar (4.24.2), in the two wives of Jacob (4.21.2), and in the two daughters of Lot (4.31.2). The older people had to be subjected to servitude through the law in order to be prepared for the coming of Christ, whereas the younger enjoyed the freedom of friendship with God.

When the Son came in the flesh, the older people (prefigured by Esau) rejected Him, but the younger one (prefigured by Jacob) accepted Him and inherited all the blessings of the older one (4.21.2; 3.21.1). While now all the pagan nations participate in God's life, fleshly Israel is excluded from inheriting the grace of God (3.21.1) and no longer possesses the Spirit (3.17.2). Yet the Church remains a union of those who were far off and those who were close, of pagans and Jews. For the two arms of Christ are extended on the cross symbolizing the two peoples dispersed to the ends of the world, who is still the head of both, uniting them to the one God through Himself (3.5.3). The Church is then for Irenaeus, the goal and fulfillment (unity) of the economy of the Old Testament: in the seed of Abraham, and the harvest of the seed sown by he Patriarch and Prophets, manifested in the reality of Christ and also in the Church—as it moves itself toward the ultimate unity—in the realization of the promises of Christ one day in the heavenly Jerusalem.[36]

iv. Trinitarian Unity— Ecclesial Unity and its Relationship to Spirit

Kereszty states that the Church is not the center of Irenaeus's theology, but "as principle that operates in every member of the Church, that again speaks for its unity as one subject of action on its diverse levels of faith ecclesial life.

As the Spirit is also the ultimate basis for the unity of the four Gospels bound together (*A.H.* 3.11.8), so then the same Spirit is the ultimate identity of the Church, as it witnesses to the truth of the Apostolic witness to the Christ, and as it constantly rejuvenates the faith of the ecclesial Church, "its container," or the structures of the Church (3.24.1). And it is the "Spirit of God" that must "dwell in their hearts through faith" (5.9.2). The Spirit becomes the immanent principle of divine life within human beings. He penetrates and transforms the flesh, "so that the flesh forgets itself and assumes the quality of the Spirit" (5.9.3). Participation in the Spirit is so real that the Holy Spirit in fact does become our spirit, completes our humanity and leads us to full maturity through the vision of God. There is still a distinction between the "Head" and the "spiritual man" which is essentially received as a gift of faith in the Church community of believers.

The Spirit does not imprint His own image to humans, but leads us to the Son. The Spirit is the agent who brings about a process of conformation to Christ as members of the body, of the Church (5.9.1; 4.37.7). "...It must share in His passion, death, and resurrection" (4.24.; 3.19.3). And through her union with Christ in the Holy Spirit the Church truly mediates salvation to the world.[37]

This dynamism of ascent to God does not stop at union with the Son, for our final goal is personal communion with the Father. The new person perfected by the Spirit, conformed to the image of the Son, ascends to the Father, becomes filled with His vision and life—and begins an eternally new dialogue of friendship with Him (*A.H.* 5.36.1; cf. 3.18.7; 5.36.2; 5.36.1).

Kereszty states Irenaeus believes the whole human race is called into this communion with the Father, through the Spirit and through the one Son *in the Church*. This in the sense that Irenaeus's perspective is so universal and so much centered on the Trinity, that it forms the center of his ecclesiology. It revolves around a focus on a renewed humanity in the Spirit, regaining the lost likeness of the Son and then reaching full perfection and maturity in communion with the Father.

Thus having surveyed Irenaeus's conception of the profound unity of the Church community states Kereszty, we can better understand his strong response to and as judge of heresy and schism. To destroy or disrupt the faith of the Church and the participation in Her life—is to weaken or not be able to participate in and be nurtured by Her life,38 since "the Spirit is where the Church is," and where we can have the truth since the Spirit is truth; and where we can have eternal life since the Spirit alone gives life (*A.H.* 3.24.1; 4.33.7).

v. *Pastoral Unity—The Paschal Controversy and Irenaeus*

Nor were Irenaeus harsh words for those who would divide the unity of the church reserved only for heretics or schismatics. Some scholars believe the strong words of *A.H.* 4.33.7 refer in part to the decision of Pope Victor to excommunicate all Churches that did not accept the Roman tradition of celebrating Easter on the Sunday following the Jewish Passover (versus the Eastern Apostolic tradition on the Sabbath). Even for the "sake of some reform" it is not worth the cause of divisions in the universal Church, "the great and glorious body of Christ," says Irenaeus. Through

Eusebius letter we know that Irenaeus also reminded Victor of the tolerant practice of his predecessors who all lived in peace with the Churches that celebrated Easter differently.39

Thus the attitude of Irenaeus on Church unity for Kereszty, is nuanced in that he never stops insisting on unity in essentials (Apostolic), but also insists on tolerating a difference in traditions which do not concern the danger of disrupting the "one and same faith." For even as he testified in other contexts to the unique authority of the Church of Rome (because of two martyrs of the faith of Apostolic status) with whom every Church agrees as representative " in matters of faith," Irenaeus can at the same time still oppose and even possibly condemn vigorously (if the above *A.H.* passage is directed against Pope Victor) the attempts of Rome to impose her discipline on the universal Church.

Precisely this full ecclesial reality of every local Church, and in particular the Holy Spirit in each of them (a real pneumatic but balanced charismatic dynamic, whose role is to make one out of many), demands an intimate union among the local Churches and proscribes any attempt to break up their communion for "a trifling reason" (*A.H.* 4.33.7). It is an ecclesial praxis of the harmony of many in the one faith, the love of God expressing itself in fraternal love, as representing the ongoing realization of the coming eternal communion in the heavenly Jerusalem. Irenaeus insistence to preserve, balance, and unify so many diverse elements of his ecclesiology as a united faith community, is of great ecumenical significance today.

NOTES

1. Heather Ward, *The Gift of Self* (Darton, Longman & Todd: London, 1990)
2. Ibid., p. 82
3. Matthew Fox, *The Coming of the Cosmic Christ* (HarperCollens: San Francisco, 1988) pp. 107-109
4. Walter Lowe, "Christ and Salvation," in *Christian Theology: An Introduction to Its Traditions and Tasks*, ed. P. Hodson (Fortress Press: Philadelphia, sec. ed. 1985) p. 226
5. Ibid., p. 4
6. Fox, p. 78
7. Ibid., pp. 87-99 (See Phil.2:1-24; Rom.8:14-39; Col.1:15-20; Eph.1:3-14; Heb.1:1-4; Jn.1:1-18; Rev.5:9-10,13-14)
8. Clarence Jordan, *The Substance of Faith* (Association Press: New York, 1972) pp. 42-43
9. Fox, p.134. See notions of 'Paradigm Shifts' in theology in Hans Kung's, *Christianity* (Continuum: New York, 1995) and David S. Bosch, *Transforming Mission: Paradigm Shifts in Theology of Mission* (Orbis Press: New York, 1977)
10. Robert N. Bellah, *Habits of the Heart: Individualism and Commitment in American Life*
    (Harper & Row: New York, 1985) p. 277-282
11. T.J.Gorringe, " 'Not Assumed is Not Healed:' The Homoousion and Liberation Theology" SJT vol. 38 no. 4 (1985) p. 481
12. Ibid. p. 482
13. Conrad Simonson, "Irenaeus and the Future of Man," in *A World More Human: A Church More Christian*, ed. G. Devine (Alba House: New York, 1973) pp. 53-67
14. A.H. 5.29.1
15. Demo. 11; A.H. 4. 33.4, 38.9
16. Demo. 11, 14; A.H. 4.39.2
17. A.H. 4.38.1,2; 2.28.1;4.39.2
18. Demo. 12, 15; A.H. 5.16.1; 5.2; 4.39.2
19. Simonson, p. 59
20. Ibid., p. 67
21. Demo.11, 12; A.H. 5.16.1, 5.2; 5.6.1; 5.19.2; 5.20.1, 5.6.1
22. A.H. 4..6.6; 5.2.2; 5.12.4
23. Simonson, pp. 63-64
24. Ibid., pp. 66-67
25. Roch Kereszty, "The Unity of the Church in the Theology of Irenaeus," Second Century 4, no. 4 (Wint. 1984): p. 202
26. Ibid., p. 203
27. This understanding of the Church begins already in Paul and continues throughout the patristic age, states Kereszty (p. 203)
28. see the A.H. reference to Malachi in 4.17.6; 18.1; 18.4
29. Kereszty, p. 205. The rule of truth main texts are found in A.H. 1.10.1; 1.22.1; 2.11.1; 2.28.1; 2.30.9; 3.3.3; 3.4.2; 3.11.7; 3.15.3; 3.16.6; 4.35.4
30. A.H. 1.10.2-3. See also W.R. Schoedel, "The Theological Method in Irenaeus," JTS, no. 35 (1984): pp. 31-49
31. Hans von Campenhausen, *Ecclesial Authority and Spiritual Power* (Stanford University Press: Cal., 10th ed. 1986) p. 162 See also chapter 5. (A.H. 4.33.8; cf. Also 3.1.1; 3.1.19; 3.3.1; 3.4.1; 3.9.9)

32. Kereszty, p. .207 He makes an interesting note that Irenaeus used different Greek words for 'the founding of a Church by an Apostle' and 'the founding of Churches in general.'
33. Kereszty states (p. 208 n. 9) that this presbyter-bishop succession is intimately connected in Irenaeus mind not only with the uncorrupted purity of the Word, but also with an irreproachable integrity of life (A.H. 26.5).
34. It is important to remember the vital role the Spirit plays with the Son in this process (Irenaeus' 'Two hands of God' idea) in facilitating this whole process, and which we will allude to later in the section on 'Unity and the Trinity'.
35. Ibid., p. 209
36. Interestingly, Denis Minns', *Irenaeus* (Georgetown University Press: Washington, 1994) in chapter 7 "From Christ to the Kingdom" states that by nature of the logic of Irenaeus eschatological reality, his emphasis is on the redemption of human embodiment (recapitulation), and Christ's return for a thousand years to banish the AntiChrist, means the establishment of a renewed earthly Jerusalem where the just will rise from the dead. So this kingdom of the just will be a social and political reality, not just a physical one. These people will not die, rather they will learn to forget to die and grow accustomed to immortality, and the vision of the Father (A. H. 5.32.1; 35.1-2; 36.2-3). At the end there will be a new heaven and earth, the heavenly Jerusalem descending to the new earth (A.H. 5.35..2; 36.1). And all will go on increasing in their knowledge and love of Him, according to their capacity (A.H. 5.36.1-2). This puts an important spotlight on the nature and role of the earthly ecclesial Church community and its life of faith as the *escaton*.
37. Kereszty, p. 214
38. Irenaeus states that the most concrete way of achieving this intimate bond between the flesh (the weak and mortal humanity devoid of divine life) and the Spirit is—the Eucharist, where the Christian proclaims the "union and communion of flesh and spirit" (A.H. 4.18.5); a precursor to the notion of the Church as sacramental, a term Irenaeus does not use.
39. G.A. Williamson, *Eusebius: The History of the Church from Christ to Constantine* (Penguin Books: Baltimore, 1965), *Eus.* H.E. V .xxiii

Conclusion

EUCHARIST AS THE ULTIMATE 'HERMENEUTICAL PRAXIS'

[T]he presbyters before you who did not observe [the *Pascha*] sent the eucharist to those from parishes who did. And when the blessed Polycarp was staying at Rome in the time of Anicetus...neither could Anicetus persuade Polycarp not to observe, seeing that he had always observed with John the disciple of our Lord and the rest of the Apostles with whom he had passed his time, nor did Polycarp persuade Anicetus to observe, who said he was obliged to hold the customs of the presbyters who were before him. But with things in this state, they were in communion with each other, and in the Church, Anicetus yielded the thanksgiving to Polycarp, with manifest respect, and they parted from each other in peace, all the Church being in peace, both those who observed and those who did not observe.

—Irenaeus to Pope Victor1

It is rather appropriate that the last correspondence we have of Irenaeus with the Roman Church is concerned with the unity of the church as it revolved around 'eucharistic observance' of liturgical unity amid diversity. It is appropriate because the eucharist for Irenaeus, and us, epitomizes or summarizes everything Irenaeus has stood for. The eucharist itself is a form of recapitulation of the gospel of Christ, focusing in on the unity of the body of Christ, the participation in, the communion of the Church. The eucharist represents the 'catholicity' of the Church at a local and universal level. It is as if the centrality of the 'great thanksgiving' is the focus of an 'ecclesial koinonia,' which in turn is actualized spiritually and materially (again for Irenaeus ideally countering the Gnostic emphasis) in an 'ecclesial liturgy.' We might say that one of the great Irenaean insights is that 'koinonia ecclesiology' is rooted in a 'liturgical ecclesiology.' That is, the 'eucharist' embodies the ultimate 'hermeneutical praxis' as the foundation of the faith ecclesial community.

This is the deepest "Apostolic" reason for the core actions of Christian worship. As the deacon Emeritus and his companions said in the midst of the persecution of Diocletian (284-305), when they were accused of participating in the Sunday assembly: "We cannot be without the supper of the Lord."[2] These things we know together have to do with our survival. The "Church" is none other than the 'assembly' that does these things together in which we encounter Christ, in which the Spirit acts. As Irenaeus would conceivably say, these concrete, real holy things connect us to a concrete, real history of the Church community. And they connect us to the concrete, real earth, in the real wine, and bread and water of baptism and service in which we encounter Jesus Christ in each other and in the Word and Eucharist.

In the last decade of the second century, Irenaeus of Lyons wrote a letter, preserved for us in the *Ecclesiastical History* of Eusebius, to Victor, the bishop of Rome. The letter, one of the most important documents of the so-called paschal controversy, was sent in the name of the Christians of Gaul as a passionate appeal for unity within an accepted liturgical diversity, an appeal against Victor's decree that the Christians of Asia, who kept a paschal fast ending on the fourteenth day of the springtime moon rather than on Sunday, were to be considered "all utterly excommunicated." As far as we know, Victor had not demonstrated why the Asian custom violated the gospel, why they constituted "heterodoxy;" they were simply not his practice, nor were they the customs of his predecessors or of many local Churches. Over against Victor, Irenaeus cited examples of ancient diversity in ritual practice that had not broken the communion (koinonia) of the Churches. Not only is this historical evidence of diverse practice in the length and times of the paschal fast but also evidence of a time when some Churches—notably the Roman Church—kept no *Pascha* at all, while other Churches had begun to do so.[3]

It is to recall Irenaeus famous dictum: "[T]he disagreement about the fast confirms the concord in the faith."[4] Irenaeus envisions a 'concord' of agreement of a liturgical or ritual unity within a liturgical diversity (even with disagreement), in examples such as our opening quote; of recalling times when earlier Roman presbyters would send the eucharist to Christians of differing calendrical practice, and the time when Anicetus of Rome yielded the thanksgiving at table to the visiting Polycarp of Smyrna.

But why was this Eucharist so important to Irenaeus? The very bread and cup of the thanksgiving meal, which are the body and blood of the Lord and which nourish our own flesh and blood, proclaim the truth of the God who created the concrete world and redeemed it in the Incarnate Christ. Encounter with the eucharist and its communal practice, forms a praxis faith in the Creator of all things and gratitude for the recapitulation for all the created cosmos. And if this is so, how could anyone whether bishop or Gnostic, not celebrate Eucharist and ignore its very meaning? In the Eucharist are assertions about the Church, about the community that celebrates the eucharist and about its relationship with the world. The presupposition here is that Irenaeus's Eucharist is the inheritance of all the Churches.

What is meant by "Eucharist" then — probably in Irenaeus, certainly here — is not just the Lord's Supper, isolated and considered one illustration of the Christian message. Rather, it is the whole economy of salvation: of Word set next to meal, texts set next to preaching, thanksgiving set next to eating and drinking, which makes up the deepest ecumenical pattern for celebration of ecclesial Christian community.

Eucharist in this sense, is also baptism as the way that leads people into the assembly, and it is mission in the world and response to the poor as ways in which the community flows out from the assembly. Eucharist is the assembly itself and its leadership, a leadership best understood as appointed for the sake of that assembly. This economy of praxis faith meaning, is as one contemporary ecumenical consultation put it, "the inheritance of all the Churches, founded in the New Testament, locally practiced today, and attested to in the ancient sources of both the Christian East and the Christian West."[5] So we see in Irenaeus that it is the whole person in ecclesial community, reflected in the eucharist, who shares in the image of God. As a contemporary theologian like Matthew Fox illustrates, in his 'creation spirituality,' it is an attempt to re-acquaint Western Christianity with the marks of such a creation spirituality in daily life:

> Christian [praxis] spirituality, then, is the rootedness of being in the world. In history, time, body, matter and society. Spirit is found there (or better, here) and not outside of these essential ingredients to human living. This means that economics and art, language and politics, education and sexuality are equally an integral part of creation spirituality. And not least of all, joy. The joy of ecstasy, and shared ecstasy in celebration. This is a non-elitist spirituality. A 'folk' spirituality one might call it. Of the folks, by the folks, and for the folks [a eucharistic analogy]. It is a spirituality as if people mattered.6

Moreover, the perception of the glory of God was not seen among the early Christians as some distant reality, involving a movement away from matter to the world of pure spirit, as the gnostics held. It was in the midst of matter and the Christian ecclesial community that God was perceived in His glory and in His provision of common grace. And nowhere is the sense of the material basis of a sacramental grace more strongly expressed than in the writings of Irenaeus against the gnostic aberrations of his day, states Kenneth Leech.7

For Irenaeus the eucharist presupposes the goodness of matter and of the physical world. It is the first-fruits of the new creation. But it also presupposes the goodness of matter and of the flesh, and their potential for growth in sanctification. Irenaeus speaks of our 'sharing in God', while introducing into the Christian vocabulary a phrase which was to reappear in various forms throughout the Eastern Fathers: 'The Son of God became the Son of Man to the end that man too might become the Son of God' (*A.H.* 3.10). The salvation and transfiguration of the body and of matter is also a preoccupation of the Eastern Fathers of the Church, as in Irenaeus, as when he links together the incarnation

A Church Fully Alive

and the reality of Christ's presence in the Eucharist:

> If the flesh is not saved, then the Lord did not redeem us with his blood, the chalice of the Eucharist is not a share in his blood, and the bread which we break is not a share in his body. For the blood cannot exist apart from the veins and flesh and the rest of the human substance which the Word of God truly became in order to redeem us.8

An equally striking feature of this eucharistic life, for Irenaeus, was its eschatological or future orientation. The celebrating communal Church looks forward to the New Jerusalem, and the greater life of the Kingdom. The incarnation of the Word signifies that the perfection of humankind is approaching its final stage, for Irenaeus. In the short remaining time, the Church must nourish and strengthen her children, especially in the prospect of martyrdom, which is the mark of her authenticity, and against the heretics who would deprive them of their inheritance (*A.H.* 3.24.1; 4.33.9-10; Demo. 94). The Eucharist is the chief means by which the members of the Church are prepared:

> How can we say that flesh passes to corruption and does not share in life, seeing that flesh is nourished by the body and blood of the Lord? We offer to Him what is His own, fittingly proclaiming the communion [koinonia] and union of flesh and spirit. As the bread, which comes from the earth, receives the invocation [epiclesis] of God, then it is no longer common bread, but Eucharist, and consists of the union of two things, an earthly and a heavenly; so our bodies, after partaking of the Eucharist, are no longer corruptible, having the hope of the eternal resurrection (*A.H.* 4.18.4-5).

Thus Irenaeus finds in the Eucharist an eloquent demonstration of the central themes of his theology; that we are fashioned for union in body and spirit—to be made in the image and likeness of God—is the whole focus of the Irenaean notion of the divine economy.

The culmination of Irenaeus's task, "the exposure and refutation of knowledge falsely so called", is an extended argument for the protection and promotion, but fundamentally of the necessity of the body's participation in the divine life and the resurrection of the dead. Since "flesh and blood procure for us life" (*A.H.* 5.14.4), Irenaeus' teaching on the Eucharist, thus reflects and supports his emphasis on the concrete praxis salvation of the whole human person—as truth. And that again fundamentally too, it is lived out (based on the *protection and guidance* of the believers praxis life of the 'rule of faith')—*in* the liturgical *and* ecclesial as *faith community.*

This calls us to embody the *whole* incarnational reality of Word and Spirit as starting there—in the supportive sacred relational womb—and then issuing outward as mission. It is then within this context that we are led to a 'sacred and wholistc lifestyle' (praxis/discipline) as a spiritual or in many ways, a transformational counter-cultural community in the world.

We are thus intended and created by God as meant to be a 'Eucharistic Thanksgiving'—in the great church transformative *mysterium* of community—broken yet blessed to be shared to feed and be nurtured as the family of God. So in turn as we offer up each other in sacred community, we as an *ecclesia*, also offer ourselves for others outside the community as we witness to the love of the Lamb of God slain for the healing of all touched by our praxis of 'Incarnational' and 'Trinitarian' love as believers. To be then shared with those who are attracted to 'come and see' (Jn. 1:39) and 'taste and see that the Lord is good' (Ps. 34:8).

The faith *ecclesial* community then becomes in God's name, if we were to paraphrase a verse from Proverbs (18:10), a 'place of protection—like a strong tower—where good people who live right praxis (or healthy life/styles) can run there and be safe.'

NOTES

1. Irenaeus, quoted in Eusebius, *Ecclesiastical History* 5:24:13
2. Quoted in Lathrope, p. 111, from the Latin text in J.-P. Migne, ed., *Patrilogiae Cursus Completus*, Series Prima 8 (Paris: 1844) p. 695
3. Thomas Talley, *The Origins of the Liturgical Year* (Pueblo Pub.: New York, 1986) pp. 20-24
4. Eusebius, *Ecclesiastical History* 5:24:13
5. "Towards Koinonia in Worship," 4, in Thomas F. Best and Dagmar Heller, eds., *So We Believe, So We Pray*, Faith and Order Paper 171 (World Council of Churches: Geneva, 1995) pp. 6-7
6. Matthew Fox, ed., *Western Spirituality: Historical Roots, Ecumenical Roots* (Fides/Claretian: New York, 1979) p. 12
7. Kenneth Leech, *Experiencing God: Theology as Spirituality* (Harper and Row: San Francisco, 1985) p. 272
8. A.H. 5.2

BIBLIOGRAPHY

Arnold, Eberland. *The Early Christians: A Sourcebook on the Witness of the Early Church.* Grand Rapids: Baker Book House, 1970.

Bacq, Philippe. *De l'anciene a la nouvelle alliance selon S. Irenee de Lyon.* Paris: Cerf, 1986.

Balas, David L. "The Use of Interpretation of Paul in Irenaeus' five books *Against Heresies*" *Second Century* 9 (Spr 1992) :27-39.

Balthaasar, Hans Urs Von, ed. *The Scandal of the Incarnation: Irenaeus Against the Heresies.* San Francisco: Ignatius Press, 1990.

Banks, Robert. *Paul's Idea of Community: The Early House Churches in their Historical Setting.* Grand Rapids: William B. Eerdmans, reprint 1982.

Baum, Gregory. "The Church Against Itself: Conflicting Ecclesiologies." *Grail* 3 (Mar 1987) :39-53.

Bellah, Robert. *Habits of the Heart: Individualism and Commitment in American Life.* New York: Harper & Row, 1985.

Berkhof, Hendrikus. *Christian Faith: An Introduction to the Study of the Faith.* Grand Rapids: Eerdmans Pub., 1985.

Bettenson, Henry. *The Early Christian Fathers.* London: Oxford University Press, 1969.

Bissonette, Tomas, G. "Comunidas Ecclesialess De Base: Some Contemporary Attempts to Build Ecclesial Koinonia." In *The Church a Community.* J.H. Provost ed. Washington, D.C: Canon Law Society of America, 24-58. 1984.

Bosch, David S. *Transforming Missions: Paradigm Shifts in Theology of Mission.* New York: Orbis Press, 1977.

Bowe, Barbara Ellen. *A Church in Crisis: Ecclesiology and Paraenesis in Clement of Rome.* Harvard Dissertation in Religion, no. 23. Minneapolis: Fortress Press, 1991.

Breck, John. *The Power of the Word.* Crestwood: St. Vladimir Seminary Press, 1986.

Brown, Raymond E. *The Community of the Beloved Disciple.* New York: Paulist Press, 1977.

Campenhausen, Hans Von. *Ecclesiastical Authority and Spiritual Power: In the Church of the First Three Centuries.* Stanford: Standford University Press, reprinted 2000.

Clark, David. *The Liberation of the Church.* Birmingham: The National Centre for Christian Communities and Networks, 1984.

Constantelos, Demetrios J. "Irenaeus and His Central Views on Human Nature" *SVTQ* 33 (1989).
──────────. "Irenaeus of Lyons and His Central Views on Human Nature" *Saint Vladimir's Theological Quarterly* 33 no. 4 (1989) :351 -363.

Culpepper, R. A. *Anatomy of the Fourth Gospel: A Study in Literary Design.* Philadelphia: Fortress Press, 1983.

De Smedt, Emile-Joseph. *The Priesthood of the Faithful.* New York: Paulist Press, 1962.

Donaldson, James, and Roberts, Alexandre eds. "Irenaeus Against Heresies" in *The Ante-Nicen Christian Library,* Vol. I. Grand Rapids: Eerdmans, reprint of Edinburgh edition, 1886-87.

Donovan, Mary A. "Alive To the Glory of God: A Key Insight in St. Irenaeus *Theological Studies* 49 (Jun 1988) :283-297.

―――――――――. "Irenaeus in Recent Scholarship" *Second Century* 4 no. 4 (Wint 1984) :219-241.
―――――――――. "Irenaeus: At the Heart of Life, Glory" in *Spiritualities of the Heart*, Annice Callahan ed. New York: Paulist Press, 1990.
―――――――――. "Insights on Ministry: Irenaeus" *Toronto Journal of Theology* 2 no. 1 (Spr 1986) :79-93.
―――――――――. *One Right Reading: A Guide To Irenaeus*. Collegeville: The Liturgical Press, 1997.

Dudley, Carl S. and Hilgert, Earle. *New Testament Tensions and the Contemporary Church*. Philadelphia: Fortress Press, 1987.

Ecclestone, A. *Yes to God*. London: Darton, Longman & Todd, 1982.

Eusebius. *The History of the Church*. Trans. G.A. Williamson. Harmondsworth, 1963.

Fahey, Micheal. "Ecclesiastical Community as Communion." In *The Church a Community*. James A. Provost ed. Washington: Canon Law Society of America, 1984.

Famier, Williaim R. "Galatian and the Second Century Development of the *reugla fidei*" *Second Century* 4 no. 3 (Fall 1985) :143-170.

Farrow, Douglas. "St. Irenaeus of Lyons: the Church and the World" *Pro Ecelesia* 4 (Sum 1995) :333-355.

Ferguson, Everett ed. *Orthodoxy, Heresy, and Schism in Early Christianity*. vol. 4 Studies in Early Christianity, New York: Garland Pub., 1993.
―――――――――. " The Kingdom of God in Early Patristic Literature." In *The Kingdom of God in 20th-Century Interpretation*,

W. Willis ed. Peabody, Mass: Hendrickson Pub., 191-208. 1987.

Fox, Matthew. *The Coming of the Cosmic Christ*. San Francisco: Harper & Row, 1988.

Gager, John G. *Kingdom and Community: The Social World of Early Christianity*. New Jersey: Prentice-Hall, 1977.

Gilliard, Frank D. "Apostolicity of Gallic Churches." *Harvard Theological Review* 68 (Ja 1975) :17-33.

Gorringe, Timothy J. "Not Assumed is Not Healed: The *Homoouson* and Liberation Theology" *Scottish Journal of Theology* 38 no. 4 (1985) :481-490.

Grant, Robert M. *Early Christianity and Society*. New York: Harper & Row, 1977.
——————. *Irenaeus of Lyons*. London: Routledge, 1997.

Greer, Rowan, A. " The Christian Bible." In *Early Christian Interpretation*. James L. Kugel and Rowan A. Greer. Philadelphia: Westminster Press, 1986.

Hall, Stuart, G. *Doctrine and Practice in Early Christianity*. Michigan: William B. Eerdmans, 1991.

Hamman, Adalbert. "Irenaeus of Lyons in Lyons." In *The Eucharist of The Early Christians*, W. Rordorf et al. New York: Pueblo Pub. Comp., 86-98. 1978.

Hammell, Patrick J. *Introduction to Patrology*. Cork: The Mercier Press, 1968.

Harakas, Stanley S. *Living the Faith: The Praxis of Eastern Orthodox Ethics*. Minneapolis: Light and Life Pub. Comp., 1992.

Hart, Trevor A.. "Irenaeus: Recapitulation and Physical Redemption." In *Christ In Our Place,* T. Hart and D. Thimell, eds. Pittsburgh: Pickwick Pub, 1989.

Hodgson, Peter C., and King, Robert H., *Christian Theology: An Introduction to its Traditions and Tasks.* Philadelphia: Fortress Press, revised 1982.

Hoskyns, E. C. *The Fourth Gospel.* London: Faber and Faber, 1947.

Jay, Eric G. "From Presbyter-Bishops to Bishops and Presbyters: Christian Ministry in the Second Century" *Second Century* I, no. 3 (Fall 1981) :25-162.

Jones, Cheslyn, Wainwright, Geoffrey, and Yarnolds, Edward, eds., *The Study of Spirituality.* New York: Oxford University Press, 1986.

Jordan, Clarence. *The Substance of Faith.* New York: Association Press, 1972.

Kee, Howard Clark. *Who are the People of God: Early Christian Models of Community.* New Haven: Yale University Press, 1995.

Kelly, J. N. D. *Early Christian Creeds.* New York: Longmanns, 1972.

Kereszty, Roch. "The Unity of the Church in the Theology of Irenaeus." *Second Century* 4, no.4 (Wint 1984) :202-218.

Kung, Hans. *Christianity: Essence, History and Future.* New York: Continuum, 1995.

Lathrop, Gordan W. *Holy People: A Liturgical Ecclesiology.* Minneapolis: Fortress Press, 1999.

Lawson, John. *The Biblical Theology of St. Irenaeus.* London: Epiworth

Press, 1948.

Leech, Kenneth. *Experiencing God: Theology as Spirituality.* San Francisco: Harper & Row, 1985.

Loewe, William. "Irenaeus' Soteriology: Transposing the Question." In *Religion and Culture,* T. Fallon and P. Riley eds. Albany: State University of New York Press, 167-179. 1987.

Lohfink, Gerhard. *Jesus and Community: The Social Dimension of the Christian Faith.* Philadelphia: Fortress Press, 1984.

Lonergan, Bernard. *Method in Theology.* Toronto: University of Toronto Press, reprint 1994.

Longenecker, Richard N. "Three Ways of Understanding the Relations between the Testaments—Historically and Today." In *Tradition and Interpretation in the New Testament,* G. Hawthorne and O. Betz eds. Grand Rapid, Mich: Eeerdmans, 22-32. 1987.

Lowe, Walter. "Christ and Salvation." In *Christian Theology: An Introduction to its Tasks and Traditions.* P. Hodson ed. Philadelphia: Fortress Press, 1985.

Lowe, P. William. "Irenaeus' Soteriology: Transposing the Question." In *Religion and Culture.* T. P. Fallon and P. B. Riley eds. Albany: State University of New York Press, 1987.

Lynch, John E. "The Limits of Communio in the Pre-Constantinian Church." In *The Church as Communion,* J. Provost ed. Washingston, D.C.: Canon Law Society of America, 159-190. 1984.

McDonald, J. Ian H.. *The Crucible of the Christian Morality in Religion. Religion in the First Centuries Series,* London: Routledge, 1998.

Meijerin, P. "Irenaeus' Relation to Philosophy in the Light of His concept of Free Will." In *Romanftas et Christianitas,* W den Boer ed. Amsterdam: North Holland Pub. Comp., 221-232. 1973.

Meyendorff, John. "Theosis in the Eastern Christian Tradition." In Christian Spirituality III, Louis Dupre and Donald E. Saliers, eds. New York: Crossroad, 1989.

Miles, Margaret. *Fullness of Life: Historical Foundations for a New Asceticism.* Philadelphia: Westminster Press, 1981.

Minear, Paul S. *Images of the Church in the New Testament.* Philadelphia: Westminster Press, 1960.

Minns, Denis. *Irenaeus.* Washington: Georgetown University Press, 1994.

Mitros, Joseph. " The Norm of Faith in the Patristic Age." In vol. VI *Church Morality and Organization in the Early Church.* E. Ferguson ed. New York: Garland Press, 1993.

Mollard, Einar. "Irenaeus of Ludunum and the Apostolic Succession." In vol. XIII *Church Morality and Organization in the Early Church.* E. Ferguson ed. New York: Garland Pub., 1993.

Moroziuk, R. P. "Meaning of KATHOLIKOS in the Greek Fathers and Its Implications for Ecclesiology and Ecumenism." *Patristic and Byzantine Review* 4 (1985): 90-104.

Norris, Richard A.. "Irenaeus' Use of Paul in his Polemic Against the Gnostics." In *Paul and the Legacies of Paul,* W. Babcock ed. Dallas: Southern Methodist University Press, 79-98. 1990.

O'Halloran, James. *Small Christian Communities: A Pastoral Companion.* New York: Orbis Press, 1996.

Osborne, Eric F. "The Love Command in Second Century Christian Writing," *Second Century* 1 no.4 (Wint. 1981) :223-243.

Pagels, Elaine. *The Gnostic Gospels.* New York: Vintage Books, 1979.

Perkins, Pheme, "Ordering the Cosmos: Irenaeus and the Gnostics." In *Nag Hammadi, Gnosticism,* C. Hedrick, R. Hodgson eds. Peabody, Mass: Hendrickson Pub., 221-238. 1986.

Piana, George La. "The Roman Church at the End of the Second Century." In vol. IV *Orthodoxy, Heresy, and Schism in the Early Church.* Everett Ferguson ed. New York: Garland Pub., 1993

Prusak, Bernard, P. "Hospitality Extended or Denied: Koinonia Incarnate from Jesus to Augustine." In *The Communion as Church,* James H. Provost ed. Washingston: Canon Law Society of America, 1984.

Purves, James J.M. " The Spirit and the Imago Dei: Reviewing the Anthropology. of Irenaeus of Lyons" *Evangelical Quarterly* 68 (Ap1996) :99-120.

Quasten, Johannes. *Patrology.* Vol. I. The Beginning of Patristic Literature, Maryland: Newman Press, 1950.

Richardson, Cyril C., ed. *Early Christian Fathers.* Vol. I. Philadelphia: The Westminster Press, 1943.

Robeck, Cecile M. "Irenaeus and the 'Prophetic Gifts.' " In *Essays on Apostolic Themes Paul* Elbert ed. Peabody, Mass: Hendrickson Pub., 104-114. 1985.

Russell, Keith A. *In Search of the Church: New Testament Images for Tomorrow's Congregations.* New York: The Alban Institute, 1994.

Ryan, Patrick. "Irenaeus and Teilhard de Chardin." In *Gospel and Word in Action* N. Brown ed. Manly, Australia, 1990 :73-78.

Schoedel, William R. "Theological Method in Irenaeus" *Journal of Theological Studies* 35 (Apr 1994) :31 -49.

Siesemann, Heinrich. "Der Begriff Koinonia in Neuen Testement Beiheft." *ZNTW* 14. Giessen, 1933.

Simonson, Conrad. "Irenaeus and the Future of Man," in *A World More Human: A Church More Christian*, G. Divine ed., 53-68. New York: Alba House, 1973.

Squire, Aelred. *Asking the Fathers: The Art of Meditation and Prayer*. New York: Paulist Press, 1973.

Stark, W. " The Sociology of Religion." In vol. V *Types of Religious Culture*. Paul Keegan ed. London: Routledge, 1972.

Starkloff, C.F. "American Indian Religion: Sacred, Secular, Human." In *A World More Human: A Church More Christian*, 69-90. New York: Alba House, 1973.

Talbert, C. N. *Reading John*. New York: Crossroad, 1992.

Talley, Thomas. *The Origins of the Liturgical Year*. New York: Pueblo Press, 1986.

Taylor, Micheal J. *A Companion to John: Readings in Johannine Theology*. New York: Alba House, 1977.

Temme, John M. "Indigenous Christologies: Perspectives from the Early Church for the Modern Church" *Trinity Seminary Review* 9 (Spr 1997) :28-39.

Theissen, Gerd. *Social Reality and the Early Christians: Theology, Ethics, and the World of the New Testament.* Minneapolis: Fortress Press, 1992.

Tillich, Paul. *A History of Christian Thought.* New York: A Touchstone Press, 1968.

Torrance, Thomas F. "The Deposit of Faith" *Scottish Journal of Theology* 36 no. 1 (1983) : 1-28.
——————. "The Trinitarian Foundation and Character of Faith and of Authority in the Church," in *Theological Dialogue* T. Torrance ed. (1985) :79- 120.

Tugwell, Simon. "The Apostolic Fathers and Irenaeus," in *The Study of Spirituality* C. Jones, Wainwright et al, 102-109. Oxford: Oxford University Press, 1986.

Unnik, William C. "Authority of the Presbyters in Irenaeus' Works." In *God's Christ and His People* J. Jervell, 248-260. 1977.

Vawter, Bruce. "John's Doctrine of the Spirit: A Summary of his Ecclesiology." In *A Companion to John: Readings in Johannine Theology.* New York: Alba House, 1977.

Voillaume, Rene. "The Glorification of the Son of Man." In *The Living God* London: Darton, Longmann & Todd, 41-53. 1980.

Wakefield, G. S. ed. *A Dictionary of Christian Spirituality.* London: SCM, 1983.

Ward, Heather. *The Gift of Self.* London: Darton & Todd, 1990.

Ware, Kallistos. "Patterns of Episcope in the Early Church and Today: An Orthodox View." In *Bishops But What Kind?* P. Moore ed., 1-21. 1982.

Ware, Timothy. *The Orthodox Church*. New York: Penguin, reprint 1985.

Williams, Rowan. "St. Irenaeus of Lyons." In *A Dictionary of Christian Spirituality*. G. S. Wakefield ed. London: SCM, 1983.

Williamson, G. A. *Eusebius: The History of the Church from Christ to Constantine*. Baltimore: Penguin Books, 1965.

Wingren, Gustaf. *Man and the Incarnation: A Study in the Biblical Theology of Irenaeus*. Edinburgh: Oliver and Boyd, 1959.
——————. "The Doctrine of Creation: Not an Appendix but the First Article" *Word and World* 4 (Fall 1984) :353-371.

Winter, David. *After the Gospels*. London: Mowbrays, 1977.

S-Yofre, Horacio. "Old and New Testament: Participation and Analogy." In *Vatican II: Assessment and Perspectives* R. Latourelle ed., 267-298. 1988.

Zizioulas, John D. *Being as Communion: Studies in Personhood and the Church*. Crestwood: St. Vladimir's Seminary Press, 1997.

ABOUT THE AUTHOR

Rick lives with his wife Melanie in Toronto and has his MA in Theology from Concordia University and M. Div from McGill University, Montreal. He is an Anglican Priest and an Associate of the Order of the Holy Cross.

His passion has been to explore 'Intentional Christian Community' past and present, and believes it is the assumption of the New Testament Gospels. Rick has been involved in Hospital Chaplaincy as well as developing the formative stages of StrongTower Skete Community (strongtower.ca) and links with the ecumenical grassroots renewal movement of New Monasticism.